LONE WOLF

LONE WOLF

THE STORY OF JACK LONDON

By ARTHUR CALDER-MARSHALL

Illustrated by Biro

DUELL, SLOAN AND PEARCE

New York

Third Printing, April 1967

Library of Congress Catalogue Card Number: 62-15477

Manufactured in the United States of America
For Meredith Press

Affiliate of
MEREDITH PRESS
Des Moines & New York

CONTENTS

LONE WOLF

BEGINNING

JACK LONDON always said that he was a boy without a boyhood. He could not remember a time when he had really enjoyed himself as a boy should. He never had any toys or games. All his clothes were made at home and when at the age of seven he had his first store-bought singlet, or vest, he refused to wear a shirt over it, because he wanted to show everyone how lucky he was.

When he grew up and began to make money, his greatest delight was in games and jokes. He had drawers full of practical jokes. When Emma Goldman, who was a revolutionary, at once very violent in what she said and very gentle as a person, came to stay with him, she was presented with a book called *A Loud Explosion*. She opened it and it exploded with a loud bang. Jack London roared with laughter.

When people came to see him Jack London produced his games, his puzzles, and his practical jokes; and everybody said what fun it was that a great writer should be so jolly.

But to understand why Jack London was like this one must begin the story with the person who was most important throughout his life.

1. THE PAPER FAN

IT WAS visiting day at the Protestant Orphan Asylum in Haight Street, San Francisco, a Saturday afternoon in late August 1876. A plain solid little girl named Eliza London was waiting with her younger sister, Ida, to see her father. She was old for her age; a lot had happened in the eight years of her life. She was one of a large family. Her mother had borne eleven children before she died of tuberculosis.

Only eight of these children were alive at the time of her mother's death. But they were more than her father could cope with despite his six feet of height, his broad shoulders, and his manly beard. He had parked the eldest children among his relatives in Iowa, planning to take only Charles, his youngest son, to California, where the doctor had said the boy might recover from a blow in the chest that he had received from a baseball. The only reason he had brought Eliza and her sister along as well was that they cried so much he hadn't the heart to leave them.

John London was not very clever. When the doctor told him to take Charles to California, he meant the hot dry climate of southern California. John London chose the raw damp climate of northern California and within a week Charles was dead.

Unable to look after his two little girls, he had placed them in the orphan asylum with the promise that when he found a suitable wife they should come home again.

Eliza was happy in the orphanage. She used to say years later that it was the happiest time of her life. There was a sense of security, which her father had never given her, and she fell in love with one of the teachers, who she dreamed would make a perfect second mother for herself and Ida. John London did not share Eliza's views. His preference went to Kate Castleton, a young singer who had made a name for herself in light opera. Eliza agreed that he might do a lot worse. Kate Castleton was lovely, talented, and attractive.

As she waited for the arrival of her father, Eliza probably wondered what news he would bring of finding them another mother. As she scanned the visitors—not for sight of her father, because he was so tall that he stood out immediately—she noticed an extraordinary-looking little woman in her thirties. She was a stranger to the place—one of the teachers was escorting her—and what made her extraordinary was not her face, which was inconspicuously plain, but her nearsightedness and the fact that she was wearing a wig, a man's wig.

Imagine Eliza's surprise when the teacher brought the little woman over to her and Ida and said, "Your father isn't very well, but this lady is a friend of his."

Imagine her horror, when the little woman said later, "I am going to be your mother."

"No!" said Eliza. "I won't believe it!"

But it was true. John London, despite his strict Methodist beliefs, had been wondering about the possibility of communicating with the spirit of his dead wife. He had begun to attend a spiritualist group and there he had met this little nearsighted woman with a wig, who went by the names of Miss Flora Wellman, or Mrs. Chaney. He was drawn to her for a number of reasons.

Flora Wellman came from the Middle West, as he did. John was from Iowa, she was from Ohio. She was of good family, the youngest of five children born to Marshall Wellman, a prosperous citizen of Massillon. Though the other children had done well for themselves, Flora had had a stormy passage. At the age of thirteen, she contracted the illness which affected her eyesight and caused the loss of her hair. Her physical growth was stunted and her balance of mind was shaken. She had moods of black despair, violent outbursts of anger, and equally violent outbursts of enthusiasm.

She had quarreled with her family and drifted toward the West Coast, making her living by teaching music, holding spiritualist séances, and doing anything else that she could turn her hand to.

At some time, she had picked up with an equally odd character, who called himself "Professor" W. H. Chaney. Chaney was an Irish-American: clever, self-educated, and irresponsible. He believed that astrology was a science—and he made a livelihood by lecturing, casting horoscopes, and writing about it. He wrote about lots of other things as well. Like so many self-educated men of his time, he was sure that he had the answers to all the important questions of his day. He was a pioneer socialist. He wrote about "The Causes and Cure of Poverty" and "What's to Be Done with the Criminal?" He was as convinced that God did not exist as he was that he could foretell the future by the position of the stars at the moment of anyone's birth.

"Prof" Chaney and Flora Wellman thought it was old-fashioned to get married. They lived together as man and wife, until Flora found that she was going to have a baby. Then there was a terrible quarrel, which ended by Flora trying (not very hard) to shoot herself and the "Professor" being run out of San Francisco as an undesirable citizen.

In January of the year in which Flora Wellman introduced herself to Eliza London as her mother-to-be, she had given birth to a baby boy. On January 14, the San Francisco *Chron-*

icle announced the event: "Chaney—In this city, Jan. 12, the wife of W. H. Chaney, a son."

So when John London first met Flora, he saw her as a gallant and unfortunate young woman (though thirty-three, she was fifteen years younger than he was). She needed a home for her son; he needed one for his daughters. She was intelligent, used to earning her own livelihood, and full of ideas about how to make money. She had the drive, which he felt that he lacked; and she had the kindness to nurse him through his illness.

On September 7, 1876, Flora Chaney, as she signed herself on the register, married John London and took her baby son to live with him in a small flat in a working-class district in San Francisco. As soon as they were settled John London went to the orphan asylum and brought Eliza and Ida home.

The thought of having the plain little nearsighted woman as a mother did not excite Eliza. But when her father showed her the baby lying in a cradle and said, "This is your new little brother," she looked down and saw that flies were crawling over his face. Typically, Flora had forgotten to buy any mosquito netting to protect him. Eliza looked round and found a newspaper. From it she made a paper fan and, sitting down beside the cradle, she began at once that service of the baby "brother" which lasted until the day, forty years later, when his ashes were buried in a casket on a hilltop above the Valley of the Moon.

2. THE STAB IN THE BACK

THE BABY who was christened John Chaney became John London on his mother's marriage. Jack, the name by which he became famous throughout the world, was a nickname he gave himself in childhood. But for convenience's sake, he shall be called Jack right from the start.

It was an odd start. Flora was not naturally a good mother and she was always worried about ways and means of earning extra money. John London was not a strong man. Jobs were hard to get, and he earned very little. By giving séances, by lecturing, and teaching music, Flora brought in money which was desperately needed.

To look after Jack, she advertised for a wet nurse. She found a perfect foster mother in a colored woman, Mrs. Jenny Prentiss, who had lost her own baby and gave to Jack all her love, care, and attention. "I cannot remember the day when my mother was not old," Jack London used to say. But from Eliza and from Mammy Jenny he received as much love and care as he would have got from the youngest and most devoted of mothers.

While Jack was looked after by these two, John and Flora London pursued the struggle to live. John went from job to job, failing sometimes through ill health but more often because in this rapidly growing city there were always too many men chasing too few jobs. Restlessly they moved from lodging to lodging, unable to pay their rent, looking for somewhere cheaper. There was seldom enough to eat or money to spare for clothes and boots.

Then a diphtheria epidemic struck San Francisco and both Eliza and Jack caught it. This was long before the time of diphtheria immunization and the disease was a killer. The two children were quarantined in the same bed, growing weaker and weaker. Eliza fell into a coma from which she woke to see Flora and the doctor standing over the bed. She thought they were talking about the illness until she heard Flora say, "Can't they be buried in the same coffin, Doctor, to save the expense?"

She never forgot—and perhaps never forgave—this remark of her stepmother. That she lived to be able to remember was due to her father. He brought another doctor in from Oakland, who had been successfully treating diphtheria by burning off the false membrane and then painting the ulcerated throat with sulphur.

When the children recovered, the London family, followed by faithful Mammy Jenny, moved across the bay from San Francisco to the suburb of Oakland, six miles away by ferry.

Once again the trek began from job to job, lodgings to lodgings. It seemed impossible to hold a job for long, so the Londons decided to start a small grocery store in a working-class district. With the shop went four rooms at the back in which the family could live.

In the notes that Jack London made for an autobiographical book, which he did not live to write, there is a description of a scene in which a little boy in the back of a grocery store hears his "father" and mother squabbling. The "father" taunts her with having a son born out of wedlock. "I was so young," the mother cries, "and he promised me a bed of roses!"

Probably these are the very words that young Jack overheard—the idea of anyone sleeping on a bed of roses being so strange that it stuck in his memory—and this was the first time that he realized that there was a mystery about who his father was. He always wrote of John London as his father, but the secret of his birth returned to plague him again and again throughout his life.

But despite this hint of something wrong, the time at the grocery store was generally happy, except for Flora. Flora was always in a hurry. John London was doing so well in the store that he ought to do better. Flora talked him into selling a half-interest to a man called Stowell. With the money Stowell contributed John London was able to take a lease on a plot of land and cultivate it as a market garden. Farming was the one thing in life for which he had a genius. He instinctively knew the heart of the soil and refused to market any but the best of his crops.

While Stowell looked after the shop, John London cultivated his garden and drove around, taking orders for his produce and buying from the farms nearby what he did not produce himself. Flora's idea might have been the foundation of a very flourishing business, if only Stowell hadn't been a crook.

One weekend John London arrived at the store from a protracted trip to find that his partner had sold him out, and done it so cleverly that although he took Stowell to law, he recovered little more than his costs.

But in some ways the loss of the shop was a blessing in disguise. John London fell back on market gardening, selling his produce to a wholesaler. The quality of his stuff gained him the highest prices; with care and caution he could have built up a good business.

Unfortunately John London still believed as firmly in his wife's "sound business sense" as she did herself. To her he entrusted the money which he earned, but instead of paying bills she bought lottery tickets which did not win prizes, and stocks and shares recommended to her by spirits from beyond, which turned out not to be worth the paper they were printed on.

Flora's remedy was that her husband should give up his small leaseholding for a bigger one of fifteen acres. He was just beginning to make a success of growing vegetables on this when Flora pushed him into leasing a seventy-five-acre farm for raising horses and potatoes. Given a few years and hard work, he might have made a success of that, but Flora impatiently rushed him into making a down payment on a ranch in the Livermore Valley. This time the idea was to plant orchards of fruit trees, groves of olives, and raise chickens for sale to hotels in San Francisco.

From a business point of view this rushing from farm to farm was madness. But what we are concerned with is the effect that Flora and John London had on young Jack. He accepted the chopping and changing of homes and jobs as a normal thing. The restlessness which he was to show when he grew up obviously came from these early years. He accepted also his mother's attitude toward money and bills. Money was made to be spent as soon as possible; but the payment of bills was to be put off, if possible, indefinitely. A fortune was waiting around the next corner.

From John London he learned a respect for the soil and a love of the ways of good farming. It was the ideal which held good for him up to the end of his life. The earth was man's heritage, and the good man left the earth richer than he found it, whatever riches he had taken from it in the form of crops.

These were things that became part of his character when he grew up; but they were not the things that impressed him at the time.

The continual moving from house to house meant that he stayed nowhere long enough to make any friends. Eliza and

Ida were so much older than he was that they almost belonged to another generation. It was as if he were an only child; and the only people with whom he could make friends were those older than himself.

"I do not remember ever receiving a caress from my mother when I was young," he said, "but I was at long intervals cheered by my father's hand laid upon my head, and his kind 'There, there, sonny!' when things went wrong."

He took no delight in being a child, and his overriding ambition was to grow up as soon as possible. The world around him seemed designed solely for the pleasure of grownups. He hated grown-up pleasures, but he felt that he had to try to like them.

This desire to be grown up first showed itself violently when Jack was only five. It was when they had moved out from Oakland to the fifteen-acre holding at Alameda. John London was plowing and Jack was given a pail of beer to carry out to his father in the field, with careful instructions not to spill it.

He found it very heavy and it kept bumping against his leg. Rather than spill it, he thought the best thing to do was to lower the level by drinking some of it. Drinking beer was a grown-up thing and all forbidden grown-up things were nice. So he bent down and took a gulp. It tasted disgusting and he would have spat it out if he hadn't been determined to show that he really was grown up.

On his way to the field he took a number of gulps of the filthy stuff, hoping each one might taste better than the last. It didn't; and by the time he reached his father (having stirred the beer to a froth to make the pail look full) he began to feel ill.

He gave the pail to his father, who drank it down and then went on with his plowing, Jack toddling by the side. Suddenly Jack stumbled and fell just behind the near plow horse.

His father yelled "Whoa" and reined in the team with a jerk, just in time to prevent the boy being killed by the gleaming plowshare.

His father carried him scarcely conscious to the edge of the field, where he lay for the rest of the afternoon, sleeping off this first attempt at being grown up.

Exactly how deep an impression this really made on Jack London as a little boy is hard to say. He wrote an account of it later in *John Barleycorn,* a book designed to expose the evils of drinking alcohol in all its forms, and it was dramatic and horrifying. But this does not prove that it was really like that at the time. One cannot even be sure that little Jack actually fell between the horses and the plowshare. Jack London the writer believed in writing *effectively* rather than *truthfully;* so perhaps it wasn't quite so tragic as he made out.

The same is true of his childhood privations. Writing of his early life to a girl with whom he was in love, he said, "Do you know my childhood? When I was seven years old, at the country school at San Pedro, this happened. Meat! I was that hungry for it I once opened a girl's basket and stole a piece of meat—a little piece the size of my two fingers. I ate it, but I never repeated it. In those days, like Esau, I would have literally sold my birthright for a mess of pottage, a piece of meat. Great God! when those youngsters threw chunks of meat on the ground because of surfeit I could have dragged it from the dirt and eaten it; but I did not. Just imagine the development of my mind, my soul, under such material conditions. This meat incident is an epitome of my whole life."

It sounds terrible—as it was meant to sound to a girl who was trying to induce him to give up the gamble of being a writer in favor of a steady job with no prospects. But when the Londons were living at San Pedro, they were growing their own vegetables, only the very best of which were sent to market. There may have been little meat, but according to his mother the whole incident arose from a time when he was hungry and stole a piece of meat out of another boy's lunch basket.

Even as a child Jack London was a natural storyteller and his imagination was always working on what he did. Living in a dream world of his own, he found it hard to understand reality.

There is another story which he told in *John Barleycorn* about the time when he was in San Pedro, at the age of seven. His mother, like many another person who has come down in the world, was very fond of boasting that she and her husband had come of true Anglo-Saxon American stock and complaining about the poor Irish streaming in from the peat bogs, the Italian dagoes, and the heathen Chinese, all of whom were ruining the United States for Anglo-Saxons in general and the Londons in particular. Each time the Londons found themselves facing financial disaster she blamed these "dirty foreigners."

Little Jack had no means of telling that this was the sort of excuse which most failures produce to excuse their own lack of success, and even when he grew up, he never rid himself of his mother's belief in the superiority of the Anglo-Saxon race, even though his stanchest friend was the Negress Mammy Jenny. When Flora told him that you could never trust an Italian, because if you crossed him he would think nothing of stabbing you in the back, the seven-year-old Jack took this literally.

Now when the Londons rented the farm at San Pedro their nearest neighbors were not Anglo-Saxons. They were peat-bog Irish and Italian dagoes; that is to say, they were scarcely human, in Jack's eyes, and very dangerous.

When the Catholic Week of the Holy Ghost came around the invitation went out to all the neighbors, whatever their race or religion, for seven days and seven nights of open hospitality. It was not a children's holiday, but the children were brought along, because they could not be left behind.

It began on an Irish ranch, with a great deal of drinking followed by drunken quarreling. Jack, who all his life was fascinated by violence, perhaps because of the violence of his mother's moods, watched the squabbles. There was a moment when it looked as if two men would kill each other. When they didn't, he was disappointed. Fighting and killing were part of the grown-up world to which he felt he should grow accustomed.

Then the suggestion was made by the younger members of the party that they should go over to the Margo ranch, which was four miles away. Margo was an Italian farmer who had married an Englishwoman who had given him a fair-haired, blue-eyed son, named Dominic; and the Margoes had their eyes on the fifteen-year-old Eliza London as a possible wife for him. Flora and John London did not go with the children; but Eliza, Ida, and Jack walked the four miles in company with other boys and girls. Jack was proud that there was a little girl of about his own age for him to squire. It made him feel grown up.

But when they reached the Margo ranch there was such a lot of noise and dancing, of horseplay on the part of the young men, and high, nervous laughter and screams from the young girls, that Jack drew on one side, knowing that however much he might pretend, he was still only a kid.

Seeing him apart, one of the Italian boys, Peter, came over and offered him half a tumbler of the raw red wine that everybody was drinking. Jack shook his head.

Peter wouldn't take no for an answer and pushed the tumbler across to him, urging him to drink. Peter had dark hair and dark eyes and Jack remembered what his mother had said about dark Italians stabbing you in the back if you crossed them. Peter had been drinking, and Jack hadn't forgotten the fight that had nearly led to bloodshed at the Irish farm. He looked around the room at all the people dancing, reeling, shouting, drinking. He did not want to be stabbed in the back, so he picked up the tumbler and gulped back the wine in one draught, as if it were medicine. It was horrible, but at least now Peter wouldn't stab him in the back.

Peter was amazed. He had never seen anyone toss back wine in that way and he called Dominic over to see the amazing feat. Then he poured out another tumbler of the wine.

Jack's fear was redoubled. Now there were two Italians

who might stab him in the back if he crossed them. Once again he downed the wine.

And so it went on, with more and more people being called to watch the feats of this prodigious child drinker.

"Had I lacked imagination," Jack London wrote in *John Barleycorn,* "had I been stupid, had I been stubbornly mulish in having my own way, I should never have got into this pickle. And the lads and lasses were dancing and there was no one to save me from my fate. How much I drank I do not know. My memory of it is an age-long suffering of fear in the midst of a murderous crew and of an infinite number of glasses of red wine passing across the bare boards of a wine-drenched table and going down my burning throat. Bad as the wine was, a knife in the back was worse, and I must survive at any cost."

When at last the party was over, Jack tried to walk home. He collapsed. "Had I been a weakling of a child," he wrote, "I am confident that it would have killed me." As it was, he was ill for days afterward.

When he recovered, his mother warned him against the dangers of alcohol. He said nothing, not daring to tell her that he had only drunk the wine in order to prevent himself being stabbed in the back. He agreed with his mother about the dangers of drinking, and the only thing that puzzled him was that other people looked on the whole incident as a joke. Drinking, according to them, was something which grownups did. And so it was something which Jack, who wanted more than anything else to be grown up, believed that he would have to learn to do, horrible as it was.

3. THE YOUNG BREADWINNER

THE SEVEN-YEAR-OLD Jack London wanted to be ordinary, to be "just like anybody else." But, like everybody else, he had his own particular talents which struggled blindly to express themselves.

His difference from the people around him showed itself in a passion for reading. There were few books in the London household, and the first to fire his imagination was a copy of Washington Irving's *The Alhambra,* lent to him by a schoolteacher. This account of the wonderful palace built by the Moors in Granada opened the door on the world of strange and beautiful things which lay across the seas. He read it enthralled, but when he returned it to the teacher he was too shy to say how much he had enjoyed it and the teacher, thinking that he had been bored, did not offer the loan of any others.

Having found that books could transport him on a magic carpet away from the worry and restlessness of his home, Jack found others in the houses of neighbors. *The Alhambra* had told him of Spain in the thirteenth and fourteenth centuries. Paul du Chaillu's *African Travels* opened up a continent still mysterious and unexplored. One day, he resolved, he would sail across the seas to see for himself the primitive life of tropical countries.

But the book that impressed him most was a romantic novel called *Signa,* by the popular woman novelist Ouida.

The last forty pages were missing, but the story as far as it went seemed to Jack to be especially written for him. The hero, who like Jack himself had been born "out of wedlock," the child of an Italian peasant girl and a wandering artist, overcame this handicap by growing up to be a composer whose music was played all over the world. The beauty of his compositions made people ignore the shame of his birth.

In later life he came to regard *Signa* as a revelation of his own career as a writer. But what he said at the time to Eliza was, "You know, Lize, I'm not ging to get married until I'm forty years old. I'm going to have a big house, and one room is going to be filled with books."

It did not work out quite like that. By the time he reached the age of forty he had married twice. And he had not one, but many rooms, filled with books. Of those books forty had been written by himself and they were on his shelves in dozens of different editions—expensive editions, cheap editions, published in the United States, Canada, and Britain, translated into every European language as well as many of the Oriental languages.

But he could not not foresee that at the age of forty he would be the most widely-read living author in the world or that his life would be nearing its end. He could not even see the disasters which were so rapidly to change the course of his boyhood.

It all sprang from Flora's hurry to make a fortune.

After three rented farms in as many years Flora prevailed on her husband to make a down payment on a farm of his own in the Livermore Valley. Eliza was now sixteen and for the last year had been running the household more or less on her own, Flora having developed a weak heart which prevented her doing anything she did not like. If Eliza could look after a family of five at the age of fifteen, there was no reason why, now that she had reached the age of sixteen, she shouldn't also look after some paying guests, thought Flora. So a widower named Shepard moved in with his three children. What they paid for board and lodging would enable John London to develop his farm more quickly.

There was plenty of land on the new farm. Orchards and olive groves were planted which in a few years' time would bring in a splendid yield with very little labor. John London plowed and planted with vegetables as large a market garden as he and the family could handle on their own; but there was still acreage to spare.

This could have been rented out as pasture, until John London was ready to cultivate it himself. But Flora was sure that more money could be made if they used the land themselves.

She went to see a hotelkeeper in Oakland who agreed to take all the eggs and poultry that John London could supply. John London had never raised chickens, but Flora pointed out how easy they were. You fed them and they laid eggs if they were hens, and you ate them if they were cocks.

When John London pointed out that they had sunk all their money in the farm and they had no cash to buy what would be needed for a chicken farm, Flora explained how easy it would be to borrow money on their interest in the farm from the bank.

Flora was "the one with a business head," John agreed and with the money raised on the farm they bought all the things that chicken farmers need, such as wire netting, hen coops, and steam-heated incubators.

For a time everything went well, and it looked as if Flora's business sense was as shrewd as she always said it was.

Then the flocks were struck by fowl pest. Those that didn't die stopped laying. The vegetables and the Shepard family were their only two sources of income.

The second of these abruptly stopped when Mr. Shepard

proposed marriage to Eliza. It was a fantastic proposal, since the eldest of Shepard's daughters was only three years younger than Eliza. But Eliza accepted, probably because she saw no end to the drudgery which her stepmother would lay on her shoulders.

To Jack the loss of Eliza, who had given him the love of a sister and a mother, came as such a shock that he must have scarcely felt the final blow, which shattered all John London's hope of making a living on the land. The interest on the mortgage fell due. With all his money tied up in olives, vines, and incubators, John London had no cash to meet the payment, and the bank foreclosed, selling John London's land and stock to recover its money.

John London was fifty-eight. He was a beaten man. His wife's wild schemes for making money had knocked the spirit out of him and he had no strength to start again on his own.

But Flora was far from being beaten. The farm had failed as a guesthouse; but back in Oakland it would be a different matter. Girls were being brought from Scotland to work in the California cotton mills. There was a fortune for anyone who would give them homes. She rented a house near the mills and arranged with the management to run it as a hostel for the mill girls. Flora and Ida ran the house. John did the shopping and Jack went to school.

At first it was a great success. The money came in regularly every week. There was no difficulty in filling the rooms. The only trouble was that the house was too small. But there was a vacant building plot next door and with her first profits Flora bought it and raised a loan with which to build a bungalow to house even more mill girls.

One might think that by now John London would have summed his wife up and insisted that he should handle the business side, banking the profits and paying the bills. But he was still dazzled by her brilliance. She was so full of schemes that he never realized that she lacked the method to carry any of them through successfully.

Faithfully every week the mill girls paid their board and lodging, and Flora promptly spent it, forgetting that she would have to pay the rent on the house and interest on the loan from the bank. It wasn't long before this thriving little business went bust and once again the Londons had to move.

Jack was only ten. If he had been older, he might have learned from his mother's mistakes. His temperament with regard to business was so like hers that he needed the lesson.

As it was, Jack had little thought for the family troubles. He had discovered that in Oakland there was a building called the public library which contained even more books than he dreamed of having when he was forty. He took out tickets for himself, and when they were insufficient, tickets for the rest of the family, so that he could gorge himself on books. The librarian, a Miss Coolbrith, soon noticed this sturdy, blue-eyed boy as an inveterate reader. She found that he was interested in adventure, travel, voyages, and discoveries, and she began to feed him the books he needed. Up to that time he had had only five real books to read. Now he tore his way through volume after volume, oblivious of the world around him, living only in the pages of his books. He made himself ill with reading, developing a sort of St. Vitus' dance.

But he was not daydreaming. In *The Valley of the Moon* he made a boy obviously modeled on himself remark, "Oakland's a good place—to get away from." Oakland was on the bay of San Francisco from which ships sailed out across the oceans, up to the sealing grounds on the edge of the Arctic Circle, across to the islands of Japan and the South Seas, Formosa, and the China coast, down into the Southern Hemisphere and to the Atlantic either west around the Cape of Good Hope or east around Cape Horn. Through the

Golden Gate, the entrance of San Francisco harbor, lay the seaways leading to the great world beyond, as rich in adventure, romance, and strangeness as any of the books on the shelves of the public library. His ambition was to go to sea, but at ten the only way he could do it was in books.

When the London family was turned out of their boarding-house, they were forced into poorer quarters not far from Mammy Jenny, to whom Jack would turn for the love and food and attention which he did not get at home.

John London could not earn enough to support the family and so, before he was eleven, Jack went to work. His mother would wake him before dawn. After a hurried and scrappy breakfast he ran down to the newspaper office to collect his newspapers. There he had to learn to stand up for himself against others bigger and stronger than he was, each of whom wanted to get away first. He did his newspaper round and then went on to school.

When school was over, he went back to the newspaper office for the evening edition, which he delivered before starting on his evening work, setting up the pins in a bowling alley. On Saturdays, when there was no school, he helped to deliver ice; and the whole of Sunday he spent in the bowling alley.

It is hard to estimate what his earnings were worth. For the newspaper deliveries he was paid $12.00 a month. The cost of living was very much lower then and $12.00 would have bought at least five times as much in those days as it would today. On the other hand, John London was out of work much of the time and there was no sort of unemployment relief. Flora's money-making schemes usually ended by making a loss, and life must have been very hard. Ida obviously found it intolerable and, like Eliza, married at a very early age. By Frank Miller, her husband, she had a son on whom Flora lavished all the love that she had withheld from her own son.

After a childhood spent in loneliness Jack London found himself plunged into a world teeming with life. Apart from his schoolmates there were the gangs of newsboys with whom he had to prove himself with his fists. He learned how to stand up for himself, and there is a story of how, when John London had been given a job in the police, he was called to stop Jack fighting single-handed against a gang of brothers. Jack took the brothers on, one after another. "Is my boy fighting fair?" John London asked. "If he is, I guess there isn't no call for me to interfere." He stepped in only when one of the brothers started to fight foul.

In this work of his, especially setting up the pins at the bowling alley and selling newspapers in the saloons, Jack saw life at its seamiest. Along the water front were sailors letting themselves go after weeks or months at sea; he saw brawls and fights that fascinated and appalled him. This drunken violence seemed pointless and disgusting; and yet these were the men who went on the voyages to distant lands of which Jack had read with such admiration and delight. If he was to grow up, he believed he had to come to terms with this and not just pretend that it did not exist. The same instinct made him never refuse a "dare," if it involved danger. He was afraid of being a coward.

There had been two different sides to his character. He had wanted to be like other people and yet he had been certain that he was different. He saw a way of reconciling them. He would be different from other people by being better; a better newsboy, a better setter-up of pins in bowling alleys, a better boxer. His might have been the motto of the song, *Anything you can do, I can do better.*

He was different from the other newsboys, because he

handed over everything he earned to his mother. They used their earnings as pocket money. The only way in which Jack could earn himself pocket money was to engage in schoolboy trade.

Cards were given away with cigarettes in those days. There were sets of boxers, railway engines, opera singers, flags of all nations. Jack collected his cigarette cards out of the gutters, the ash trays in the saloons, from the customers in the bowling alleys. They formed his own personal capital, which he did not have to hand over to his mother.

Starting with cigarette cards as currency, he swapped them for postage stamps, stones, curios, birds' eggs, and marbles. He acquired the finest collection of agate marbles he had ever seen a boy possess. The core of it was a handful worth at least $3.00, which he had taken as security for a loan of twenty cents to a messenger boy, who was sent to reform school before he could redeem them.

He would swap anything for anything else, his sense of money values being far shrewder because he had no spending money of his own. If he was going to be a trader, he would be a better trader than any of them. He could not shine by spending money, so he shone by hoarding it. He became the prize miser. There wasn't a boy who could drive a harder bargain, and when the other boys collected bottles, rags, old iron, or gunny sacks, they called Jack in to drive the bargain with the junkman and paid him a commission on it.

Jack wasn't a miser for greed's sake. John London, on the rare occasions when there was a little money to spare, had taken him out in the bay, sailing and fishing. The beaten old man and the unbeaten young boy had come to enjoy each other on these excursions, when they could get away from Flora, with her hysterical outbursts and fits of rage.

From these trips on the bay Jack had conceived the ambition of buying a boat of his own. The sea drew him as strongly as the public library. Books and boats were the two legs on which he walked toward his destiny.

By the time he was thirteen he had accumulated two dollars from his private trades. With it he bought a boat that had no centerboard and leaked like a sieve. But he could run it up and down the estuary and even learned to take it for short sails across the bay, baling as he sailed and steered. It was the beginning of the training that made Jack London one of the most daring and skillful sailors of small boats of his generation.

Jack was quick to learn at school, eager to acquire any knowledge that would help him. But this did not prevent his falling foul of the singing mistress. Every day there was a quarter of an hour's singing practice, during which she noticed that Jack did not open his mouth.

When she asked him why, he answered that she sang flat and he did not want to ruin his voice.

The mistress was furious, because the answer, if true, was all the more insulting. She went straight to the principal and reported Jack for impertinence.

When Jack was hauled up to explain his impertinence, the principal obviously agreed with the boy's judgment, because he sent Jack back with a note to say that he was excused from singing, and during the singing period every morning he would write an English composition. Jack claimed that the discipline of writing a daily composition to order taught him to be able later on to write his daily thousand words wherever he was, even at sea in a storm.

Jack left this school as the star pupil. He was chosen to give the graduation speech on behalf of all who were leaving. But he refused to do so on the grounds that he had no clothes in which he was fit to be seen on the platform.

There were other, deeper grounds. The other boys and girls were going on to high school and then, if they were good enough, to university. He felt he could not bear to tell others that for him there would be no high school, no university, despite his brilliance. John London could no longer earn enough to support the family; so on Jack fell the task of earning money by whatever odd jobs he could pick up.

4. PRINCE OF THE OYSTER BAY

FOR THE next year Jack London was a typical ragamuffin hanging round the Oakland water front. He continued with the newspaper rounds, the ice round, and setting up pins in the bowling alley; and in addition to this, he did odd jobs around the saloons, scrubbing the barroom floors in the mornings, running errands, alert for anything that would turn a few cents.

Somehow or other out of his private trades he accumulated $6.00 to buy a secondhand skiff, $1.75 to give her a coat of fresh paint, $2.00 for a sail, and finally $1.40 for a pair of oars. Then the bay was wide open to him. He would steal every hour he could from his odd jobs, sailing out to Goat Island to fish for rock cod and coming back on the flood with food for the family and perhaps a little extra to sell for cash.

Sailing in the bay can be very dangerous. Currents are treacherous and squalls sudden. But Jack was utterly without fear at sea, and he would take his skiff out in weather that older, wiser sailors warned him was suicide. His luck held, and with every narrow escape his skill and daring increased.

Those few months after leaving school were happy; and they weren't such a waste of time as they might have appeared to the teachers in the high school which he should have been attending. Jack was building up his bodily strength. He was learning self-confidence and how to rely on his own judgment, the coordination of hand and eye and brain.

But then a fresh blow fell. John London was knocked down by a train and injured so badly that he was unable to work for months. The burden of the family fell entirely on Jack. The time for odd jobs and puttering with the skiff was past. He had to look for a steady job, which would bring in a regular wage.

He was only a boy and without any skill. The best job he could find was in a cannery which had been set up in a broken-down stable. His wage was ten cents an hour and he never worked less than ten hours a day. Some days he worked eighteen or even twenty hours, if there was a glut of fish for canning. His life became a treadmill of drudgery. For weeks on end he would work up to eleven o'clock every night and then walk home, to save the carfare. It was half past twelve before he flopped into bed, and five hours later his mother would have to shake him awake to go back to work.

Jack London described this terrible time in a short story, "The Apostate," published in the collection *When God Laughs*. The boy and the mother in that story were himself and Flora.

> She got a grip of the bedclothes and tried to strip them down; but the boy, ceasing his punching, clung to them desperately. In a huddle, at the foot of the bed, he still remained covered. Then she tried dragging the bedding to the floor. The boy opposed her. She braced herself. Hers was the superior weight, and the boy and bedding gave, the former instinctively following the latter in order to shelter against the chill of the room that bit into his body.
>
> As he toppled on the edge of the bed it seemed that he must fall headfirst to the floor. But consciousness fluttered

up in him. He righted himself and for a moment perilously balanced. Then he struck the floor on his feet. On the instant his mother seized him by the shoulders and shook him. Again his fists struck out, this time with more force and directness. At the same time his eyes opened. She released him. He was awake.

"All right," he mumbled.

In Jack London's story the boy has a nervous and physical breakdown. Even when he recovers his bodily strength, he refuses to go back to work for his mother and his young brother Will. "You never brung me up," he says. "I brung myself up, Ma, an' I brung up Will. He's bigger 'n me, an' heavier, an' taller. . . . Will can go to work, same as me, or he can go to hell, I don't care which. I'm tired." And off he goes to the freedom of the road, bumming his way across America on the railroad tracks.

Jack London himself reached the point of near collapse in the cannery, but he did not leave his family in the lurch—at least not then. He saw that working in the fish cannery at ten cents an hour would get him nowhere. He compared that sort of existence with the life of the men he saw on the water front when he was tinkering with his skiff. Some were sailors from ocean-going craft. One day, he resolved, he would be a sailor, but at fifteen he was too young for that. Others were sea poachers, raiding the oyster beds in San Francisco Bay and selling their plunder to the water-front saloonkeepers. It was dangerous. They risked losing their lives, if caught by a storm, or their liberty, if caught by the Fish Patrol; but they made more in a night than he made in three weeks at the cannery. They had leisure and fun and adventure. Although younger than any of these oyster pirates, Jack felt that at fifteen he was not too young to make a start.

Raiding the oyster beds was against the law, but Jack had little respect for laws that allowed little boys and girls of eight to be put to work in factories at a penny an hour. The law, as he saw it, was to keep the rich rich and the poor poor. If he thought about the danger, he would have said that he preferred to die young through drowning or a coastguard's bullet rather than through overwork and undernourishment.

Not that his thoughts were turned to death. It was adventure, romance, the excitement and wages of daring he wanted. His head was filled with tales of old voyagers, his vision with tropic isles and far horizons.

Down on the water front Jack heard that French Frank wanted to sell his sloop, the *Razzle Dazzle,* for $300. This might seem a fortune to a boy earning between six and ten dollars a week. But Jack was his mother's son, when it came to money. With the *Razzle Dazzle* he could earn $25.00 a night or more as an oyster pirate. Instead of looking at the cost of the sloop as three thousand hours' work at the cannery, Jack saw it as twelve nights' work as an oyster pirate; and cheap at the price.

The only person in his narrow world who owned $300 and had the love and trust to lend it to him was Mammy Jenny. Jack went to see her and told his story, and the very next Sunday took his skiff and rowed out to the *Razzle Dazzle.* He had the money with him and hoped to buy the sloop there and then.

But French Frank was entertaining guests; and besides, he never did business on a Sunday. He would make out a bill of sale and meet him tomorrow at the Last Chance Saloon; but meanwhile Jack must go below and meet his friends.

Jack went below, and while French Frank poured a tumbler of the red wine Jack hated out of a demijohn he was introduced to Frank's friends. There was a young oyster pirate, "Whisky" Bob, aged sixteen, and a "black-whiskered wharf rat of twenty," named "Spider" Healey. Besides them there were three women, a Mrs. Hadley and two girls, Tess and Mamie, "Spider's" nieces. Mamie was known along the water front as "Queen of the Oyster Pirates." French Frank, a man of fifty-five, was in love with Mamie; but although he had asked her to marry him often enough, Mamie would have none of him.

Jack knew nothing of this. He had only two concerns in the world: the sloop herself which would be his own next day and the foul red wine, which he could not refuse.

He acquitted himself as he thought a man should. He drank a little of the wine, but managed to pour the rest of it away when nobody was looking; and he fixed to take on "Spider" Healey as crew next day. "Spider" knew the ropes and could show him how to make the raids.

It wasn't until next day after the sale was completed that Jack realized that Mamie, the "Queen of the Oyster Pirates," had taken a fancy to him and included herself in the crew of the *Razzle Dazzle*. And even then he did not realize that French Frank, wild that his girl had been taken from him by a boy forty years younger than he was, had sworn that he would "get" Jack sooner or later.

Jack found himself in a new world which hitherto he had only glimpsed from the outside. It was a world in which everyone had a nickname. There was Nicky the Greek, "Whisky" Bob, "Spider" Healey, the Clam, Big George Nelson, and his son Young Scratch Nelson, a "reckless maniac, twenty years old with the body of a Hercules," named Scratch for the wildness with which he fought in his frequent brawls. Around their exploits hung a cloud of romance. They were desperate men. Many of them had already served a term or terms in the penitentiary. All knew they would end up there sooner or later, unless death caught up with them first.

They would put out together in a fleet of a dozen sloops, and make for the abandoned oyster beds from which they could later pretend they had taken their catch, if challenged by the shore police. Then under cover of darkness they would move toward the cultivated beds they planned to raid. Off these they would anchor the sloops and row their boats, leaping overboard and pushing them through the mud where the water was too shallow. Reaching the picking grounds, they would seize sacks and fill them as quickly and quietly as possible to avoid detection by the guards.

During the raid the pirates worked as a team, ready to defend one another if any were attacked. But the moment they were away, a race developed between them to see who could reach home first and scoop the cream of the market.

All of them were armed in some way or other, with shotguns, knives, or revolvers; and it was under cover of darkness that the pirates would pay off old scores.

One night Jack saw a sloop bearing down on him. As it came close, he saw it was French Frank's. Jack grabbed his shotgun and held the *Razzle Dazzle* on her course with his feet on the wheel. It was a test of nerve, and Jack won it. It was French Frank who had to veer away.

Jack's courage, his skill with a craft, and his daring compelled admiration from older, rougher men, who might otherwise have resented his education such as it was, his book reading, and liveliness of mind. He took big risks to reach the quay first, but he never ran aground.

Of all the pirates Jack most admired Young Scratch Nelson for his great strength and his superb handling of sailing craft. He hero worshiped him from afar, until one morning Young Scratch hailed him outside the Last Chance with an invitation to have a drink.

Jack's only craving at this time was for sweets. He would

buy a bag of them and, hiding himself in the cabin of the *Razzle Dazzle*, gorge himself.

But he could not resist an invitation to have a drink with his hero. There was so much that Jack felt he could learn from a man of Young Scratch Nelson's experience. So they went into the Last Chance and Nelson ordered two schooners of beer and they talked about raids, patrolmen, and who it could have been that put a load of buckshot through the *Annie's* mainsail.

They finished the beer and Jack waited for Nelson to suggest that they should go. But he ordered another round; and after that a third and a fourth and a fifth and a sixth. Jack was appalled at the extravagance, because each of these rounds cost as much as he had made in an hour working in the cannery. He hated the taste of the beer, but for the sake of Nelson's company he put up with it.

After the sixth beer Jack could stand no more. He made the excuse that he wanted to go aboard the *Razzle Dazzle*, which was lying at a wharf nearby.

He walked along the quay, slightly fuddled by the beer and completely perplexed by the fact that Young Scratch Nelson should have given him not one schooner of beer, but six in succession.

Suddenly the light dawned. Of course! Nelson had expected him to buy a drink in return; and when he didn't, his hero and gone on treating him, just to see when, if ever, he would!

He sat down on the springer chain between two posts on the quayside and buried his face in his hands. The heat of shame burned up his neck into his cheeks and forehead. He had blushed many times in his life, but never so terribly as this time. The two different worlds in which he had lived came into collision, the world of the cannery in which a man earned lawfully a dollar for a ten-hour day and the world of the pirates in which he earned illegally $25.00 a night. In the cannery he had sweated, scrimped, and scraped, and there was nothing to show for it. Now he was with men he admired. Could he live among them and still keep the thrifty habits that had made the newsboys hail him as the prince of misers?

"Which was it to be?" he wrote in *John Barleycorn*. "I was aware that I was making a grave decision. I was deciding between money and men, between niggardliness and romance. Either I must throw overboard all my old values of money and look upon it as something to be flung about wastefully, or I must throw overboard my comradeship with these men."

He went back to the Last Chance and found Young Scratch Nelson standing outside.

"Have a drink," Jack said.

"I had to go aboard to get some money," he explained as he paid for the two drinks.

"You didn't have to do that," Young Scratch said. "Johnny'll trust a fellow like you—won't you, Johnny?"

"Sure," agreed Johnny Heinhold, the saloonkeeper.

Young Scratch had a reckoning in Johnny's ledger and straightaway Jack decided that he must have one, too, just to prove that he was one of the boys. And when Nelson left saying that he had had enough, Jack went on to drink with Clam and Spider and Pat, the Queen's brother, and whomever else he could pick up.

Jack London always regarded this as one of the deciding moments in his life; and in this he was right. But it would be true to say it was the decisive *mistake* of his life. He posed the choice as between money and comradeship, between hoarding money like a miser or flinging it about wastefully. He was an all-or-nothing man. He could not recognize the possibility of standing Nelson a few drinks and using the rest to repay Mammy Jenny the money she had loaned him.

Once he accepted the idea of drinking beer and wine and whisky, this fifteen-year-old boy would admit no moderation. To prove that he was as good as his elders he had to drink as much as any of them or more—and stay sober. If spending was the order of the day, then he must spend more than anyone. His boyhood was over, and as evidence of this he sent a note to his mother to give away all his collections, even the marvelous agate marbles. It didn't matter to whom she gave them just as long as she got rid of them.

It wasn't long before Jack earned his nickname. Like most of the water-front nicknames, there was a mocking undertone to it. "Prince of the Oyster Bay." The connection with Mamie, the Queen, suggested it. His youth made him not the King, but just the Prince; and he won the title not so much by his exploits on oyster raids as from the princely way in which he flung his money around.

This wildness of Jack's sprang from the fact that he was shy and sensitive. He wanted to hide this beneath a mask of toughness. With a few drinks in him the shyness fell away.

"Can I ever forget the afternoon I met 'Old Scratch,' Nelson's father? It was in the Last Chance. Johnny Heinhold introduced us. That Old Scratch was Nelson's father was noteworthy enough. But there was more in it than that. He was owner and master of the scow schooner *Annie Mine,* and someday I might ship as a sailor with him. Still more, he was romance. He was a blue-eyed, yellow-haired, rawboned Viking, big-bodied and strong-muscled despite his age. And he had sailed the seas in ships of all nations in the old savage sailing days."

It is hard to say how much Jack understood what he was reaching out for. He had no thought at the time that he would ever be a writer; but he was already drinking in the innumerable yarns and scenes and characters which were to be useful to him when he came to write. The way it appeared to him, looking back at this time, was that it "was life raw and naked, wild and free—the only life of that sort which my birth in time and space permitted me to attain. And more than that. It carried a promise. It was the beginning. From the sandspit the way led out through the Golden Gate to the vastness of adventure of all the world where battles would be fought for high purposes and romantic ends."

These were the dreams that in the century before had led the pioneers from the Atlantic Coast across the plains and Rocky Mountains to the Pacific Coast. These were the dreams that had fired the great explorers in the sixteenth century to colonize the Americas and the West Indies. Jack London, in a way, was unlucky to be born too late for the high adventure for which his spirit yearned.

But the sailors and pirates on the Oakland City wharf could not see the dreams that filled the boy's mind. All they saw was a tough fifteen-year-old kid who was punishing his fine body with alcohol at a speed that appalled even those hardened drinkers.

Luckily there were the times at sea when Jack did not touch a drop. He had no taste for the stuff, and the excitement of raiding and sailing in any weather gave him a far greater thrill than the times ashore.

For months Jack sailed the *Razzle Dazzle* and despite the money he squandered found enough to repay Mammy Jenny and provide for his family. Then there was a terrific fight among the pirates. Young Scratch Nelson was shot through the hand and the *Reindeer,* his sloop, was run aground and ripped open. Jack fell foul of Spider Healey, who set fire to the mainsail of the *Razzle Dazzle* and escaped overboard. A gang of pirates clambered on to the *Razzle Dazzle,* set her on fire, stove a hole in her timbers, and sank her.

To lose the *Razzle Dazzle* was a disaster, but it was offset by the benefit of losing Spider, whom Jack had never liked. As a result, he teamed up with his hero, Young Nelson, who "could sail, even if he did frighten every man that sailed with him." Together they patched up the *Reindeer*, they borrowed from Johnny Heinhold enough money to outfit her with food, and then they sailed for Benicia well away from the Oakland gangs.

Between the sea and the Sacramento and San Joaquin rivers, which flow out through the Golden Gate, there are three lagoons, or bays: the San Francisco Bay closest to the Pacific Ocean, San Pablo Bay in the middle, and Suisun Bay reached from San Pablo through the Carquinez Straits through which a rip tide ebbs and flows. Benicia is a town at the seaward end of Suisun Bay, with opportunities for poaching quite as rich as Oakland.

Jack and Nelson divided their time between poaching and the saloons of the Benicia water front. Inevitably the time ashore grew longer and longer. Trying to keep up with Nelson drove Jack down and down. For three weeks there was not a moment when he was sober.

After one bout, at one o'clock in the morning, he reeled back to the sloop, having lost Nelson somewhere some time during the evening. He staggered, stumbled, reached out for a handhold, and found himself in the water.

The tide was in full ebb, tearing down the straits with the speed of a millrace. There was nobody on the wharf to see him, nobody aboard the sloop. Jack was so sodden with alcohol he could not reason. To be in the water, swept seaward on the tide, seemed a marvelous adventure, the first good, clean thing that had happened in weeks. He was a good swimmer and the water was delightfully refreshing to his heated blood. He just lay there, carried on the current. He was so drunk that he was not worried, even when he realized

that he was helpless and could not make the shore. The phrase came to him, "To go out on the tide." It was the best thing. In the months of his drunkenness he had seen old men wrecked by alcohol, shattered in body, and living only for the next drink. The sight had shocked him. Far better to go out on the tide.

In the way that drunken men do, he began to feel sorry for himself. It was sad, he felt, he should die so young. It made him weep for a while. But then he began to think that really he was a hero, and there was nothing sad about dying a hero's death. He began to sing his death chant.

Then he heard the gurgle and splash of current riffles which warned him of danger worse than death by drowning. Below Benicia, where the Solano wharf stuck out, the straits widened into what was called the Bight of Turner's Shipyard. He was in the shoretide that swept under the Solano wharf and then on into the bight. He knew the power of the suck that developed when the tide swung around the end of Dead Man's Island and drove straight for the wharf. Death by drowning seemed beautiful. But he did not fancy death battered against the piles of the wharf.

He undressed and struck out, crossing the current at right angles with strong over-arm strokes. He could judge his position by the wharf lights and he did not stop until he was sure that the current would carry him safely beyond the end of the wharf. Then he turned over and rested, recovering his breath after the hard swim. His body was good, but his condition was poor.

When he regained his breath, he began his death chant once more. But he stopped as suddenly as he had started, because he remembered that on the Solano wharf they worked night shift. Railroad men might hear him singing and row out and prevent him going out on the tide, and that seemed to him such a romantic thing to do.

He lay on his back in the starlight, watching the lights go by, the red, green, and white, saying good-by to them as they passed. He did not begin singing again until he was in mid-channel, well clear. Sometimes he swam a stroke or two, but mostly he floated and dreamed sad dreams of going out so young on the tide.

Before it was dawn, cold and the passage of time sobered him enough to make him wonder exactly in what part of the straits he was, and whether the tide would not turn and carry him back before he reached San Pablo Bay.

Still later he became completely sober. He was very tired and very cold. With the chill, he realized that he was going to drown. Now that he was sober, that was the last thing he wanted. He looked around. He could see Selby's Smelter to the left on the Contra Coasta shore and the Mare Island lighthouse. He tried to strike out for the Solano shore on his right, but he soon gave up. He was too cold and tired to swim. It was better to float, using his strength to keep afloat with a stroke or two in the tide rips that were gathering violence.

The reasons for living poured back on him. But the more reasons he thought of why it was sweet to live, the more certain it seemed that he was going to drown. He became very frightened.

When dawn broke behind him, he was in the tide rip off the Mare Island light. At this point the swift ebbs from the straits pouring either side of the island were fighting with one another and with the incoming flood tide driving up from San Pablo Bay. A stiff westerly breeze had sprung up and drove crisp little waves into his face. It was hard to breathe.

He had been in the water for four hours. Fatigue and cold had so weakened him that he knew he could not hold out much longer.

But at that moment he saw a boat. He shouted. He waved an arm. It was a couple of Greek fishermen from Vallejo returning with their catch. They were dark-haired, dark-eyed (the sort of people his mother had warned him against), but one of them turned the boat and leaned over and pulled the boy out like a dying fish.

5. BEYOND THE GOLDEN GATE

THAT NEAR escape from drowning was something that he never forgot. He used the incident in three different books, in three quite different ways, but always to show a complete change in a man's life.

The change that it effected in his own life was to decide him against trying to fight society as an outlaw. He still wanted adventure and romance and more money than he would ever get working with his hands as an unskilled laborer. But he foresaw that there was no future as a sea poacher or an oyster pirate. Young Scratch Nelson ended his young days in Benicia with a bullet through his Viking's head. Clam and Whisky Bob were stabbed to death; Spider and Nicky the Greek were jailed for life in San Quentin Prison for major crimes.

This is the explanation of the startling change in Jack London's life. A few days after his escape from drowning Jack and Nelson were coming back from an oyster raid when they were approached by a state officer who suggested that they should become deputies for the Fish Patrol. There was no pay, but the deputies were given half the fines of any poachers they captured.

It was a case of the Robbers turning Cops. Neither Jack nor Nelson felt any loyalty to the oyster pirates who had sunk the *Razzle Dazzle* and run the *Reindeer* aground. Nelson perhaps had wanted revenge. Jack wanted experience, and the Fish Patrol brought him more money than he had earned in the cannery, as much excitement as he had had in raiding the oyster beds, and the reassurance of working within the law.

He hadn't felt that there was anything morally very wrong about stealing oysters from private oyster beds. At least it was doing no harm to nature. But the methods of the Chinese shrimp fishers outraged him. They sank great bag nets to the bottom, where the tide ebbed and flowed. These nets were very effective for catching shrimps, but the mesh was so small that the tiniest fishes, little newly-hatched things not a quarter of an inch long, could not pass through. The beautiful beaches at Point Pedro and Point Pablo, where the shrimp fishers lived, were made foul with the stench of millions of tiny fish killed by the Chinese in their pursuit of shrimps.

He equally deplored the "Chinese line" invented by the Chinese, but used also by other poachers. By a simple system of floats, weights, and anchors, thousands of hooks, each on a separate leader only a few inches apart, were lowered as a hooked screen between six inches and a foot above the bottom of the bay. These hooks were barbless and unbaited; they were filed to a long point as sharp as a needle. A Chinese line might stretch for four hundred yards across the bottom, a formidable obstacle to the sturgeon, which goes rooting for its food like a pig.

Pricked by the first hook it touched, the sturgeon gave a startled leap and caught itself in half a dozen more. Filled with panic, it lashed right and left, getting entangled firmer and firmer, until it finally drowned. Chinese line fishing had been forbidden by the Californian Fish Laws because it was threatening to exterminate the sturgeon altogether.

Jack considered that these crimes against nature were morally far worse than raiding private oyster beds; and for some months he enjoyed working with the patrol.

But then a new excitement came his way. He had run the flood tide from Benicia up Suisun Bay to Sacramento. There he went swimming in the river and fell in with a gang of boys sunbathing on a sandspit. They talked a different language from the boys he knew, and he found that they were road kids, boy tramps who traveled the States, riding in or under freight cars, begging ("battering the main stem for light pieces," they called it), robbing or "rolling" drunks, and so on. Jack was fascinated by their language, their talk of bulls, shacks, strong arms, bindle stiffs, and punks.

These road kids presented Jack with the old challenge. "Whatever you can do, I can do better." He joined up with them, was arrested in a street fight, and served three days in jail with them.

Jack was nicknamed Sailor Kid, and was initiated into the rules of the road. He learned that he would be a "gay cat" or tenderfoot until he had ridden "the blinds" (that is, between one truck and another) over the Sierra Nevada. After that he would be a fully-fledged "punk." So one night Jack and another gay cat, nicknamed French Kid, waited in the darkness ahead of the Central Pacific Overland. As it passed they "nailed the blinds," jumping up and climbing between two cars. Jack succeeded. French Kid lost his grip and fell with a scream as the carriage wheels amputated both his legs. Whether he died, Jack never knew.

Bob, the leader of the push, had told Jack to "deck her" (riding on the top of the car), until the train passed Roseville, where the constable was "horstyle" (hostile), and then to climb down to the blind behind the mail car. Jack was too terrified to climb along the roof of the express into the cover of the blind after he had seen what had happened to French Kid, so he rode all night across the snowy Sierras, pressing low as the train passed through tunnels.

This was a piece of cowardice he kept to himself when he

rejoined the push at Sacramento. He was renamed Frisco Kid, and for some weeks he went with the push in Sacramento, a real punk.

Then he grew bored, and rode a freight car back to Oakland to see his family. He had taken to oyster raiding ostensibly in order to make money to support Flora and John London. But somehow in Benicia and Sacramento the sense of responsibility had been forgotten. He had been working out his own destiny in a blind fashion. And now the time had come for him to venture beyond the Golden Gate. He began to look for a ship.

He found what he wanted in the *Sophie Sutherland,* an eighty-ton schooner bound for Japan, Korea, and Siberia, scheduled for ninety days of harpooning, in what proved to be one of the last seal hunts to sail from San Francisco.

Jack was seventeen years and eight days old when on January 20, 1893, he signed the articles of the *Sophie Sutherland* before the shipping commissioner. He ought to have described himself as "a ship's boy," since he had had no experience in an ocean-going craft. But he signed on as "an able-bodied seaman" because the wages were higher.

The other able seamen, Scandinavians for the most part, were fully qualified men, who had served their time as ship's boys. They looked at Jack with suspicion. He might be tough and strong, but they knew that he was jumping promotion. They were prepared to be merciless if he was unequal to the job.

What they did not know was that Jack was used to challenging older men and holding his own with them. He sprang to his orders. He pulled on a rope with the best. He was first of the watch on deck and the last below. The *Sophie Sutherland,* a three topmast schooner, was a very different craft from sloops like the *Razzle Dazzle* and the *Reindeer.* But Jack was quick to learn the differences, new ropes and their names, the routine of the larger ship, how to box the compass.

On the third day out the *Sophie Sutherland* ran into a storm, the wind fierce, the sea running strong. It was Jack's turn at the wheel.

As well aware as any that Jack had signed on on false pretenses, the captain stood by as Jack took the wheel. He said nothing. He just stood and watched. Jack knew that he was being tested. If he made a mistake, he would be degraded to ship's boy immediately. But he was not nervous. The *Sophie Sutherland* was a bigger ship on higher seas than any he had navigated. But it was not more dangerous than the leaking skiff he had sailed at thirteen, bailing as he went. He watched the captain out of the tail of his eye. After a few minutes the old man nodded approval and went below.

Jack never forgot the hour he kept the *Sophie Sutherland* on her tack through that storm without another hand on deck, the sense of power in having the swift, full-sailed ship and the lives of the crew in his hands. It was the triumph of the skill he had gained as a boy in the bay.

After that there were no more dirty looks. He was accepted by the others as an able-bodied seaman, worth the higher wage.

He made two friends in the fo'c's'le. One was a Swede named Victor, the other a Norwegian called Axel. They were nicknamed The Three Sports.

Although these were his friends, he had eyes for all aboard. He had read *Moby Dick* and though the *Sophie Sutherland* was out to hunt seals, not whales, he measured her captain and crew against Captain Ahab, Pequod, and the crew of Herman Melville's masterpiece. He lived in the two worlds of literature and life; and from this voyage he was to make a novel, *The Sea Wolf,* just as he made *The Cruise of the Dazzler* and *Tales of the Fish Patrol* from his experiences on the *Razzle Dazzle* and the *Reindeer*.

The voyage with the *Sophie Sutherland* was important to Jack London in a number of different ways. It proved to him that he could hold his own among the world of men. His exploits in Oakland, Benicia, and Sacramento had been kid stuff. Even his hero Young Scratch Nelson, for all his daring, was a hoodlum, destined to end on a mortuary slab. The officers and crew of the *Sophie Sutherland* were members of organized society; and Jack's instinct was to outdo *them*, just as he had outdone the oyster pirates and the road kids.

The voyage gave him his first sight of the foreign countries about which he had read and dreamed, of Hawaii, Japan, and Korea. But he realized that next time he did not want to see them as an able-bodied seaman, calling for a day or two at a port and getting little farther than the waterside taverns. In Yokohama he caught sight of educated Americans, Europeans, and Japanese with their fine ladies. It was with them that he felt he belonged and not with Mamie, Queen of the Oyster Pirates, and girls who worked in factories and along the water front, who flung themselves at him because he was husky and good-looking.

So when he returned to Oakland from this first voyage beyond the Golden Gate he did not look around for another ship. He had had his fill of adventure for the moment. He had seen how men who had spent years roaming around the world were as ignorant as when they set out, merely because they had not had the education to digest their experience. The important thing for him now was somehow or other to make up the years he had lost by not attending high school.

But he found his family in dire straits. They had reached the end of their credit with the shopkeepers and were living on John London's meager wages as a police constable. There was no possibility of Jack's going back to school. When he had bought himself some cheap civilian clothes, paid off the debts with the shopkeepers and the landlord, there was little enough to turn over to his mother. He had to start to look for a steady job.

He couldn't have chosen a worse time. In 1893 there were eight thousand bankruptcies, including those of many banks. Any man with a job was considered lucky, however low the wages. The best he could get was work in a jute mill, where he was paid ten cents an hour, the same as he had received at the cannery as a raw boy just out of school. For a sixty-hour week he earned $6.00; and beside him were working children of eight years old and upward, earning only $2.00 for a week as long as his. All these young boys and girls were suffering from rickets and undernourishment; and many were crippled or tuberculous.

Jack felt desperate. What sort of world was it that put children to work at eight and paid a hearty young man of eighteen no more than he had earned as a boy of thirteen? He was a hard and willing worker, but he wanted an incentive, some assurance that his work would better his condition. Something was very wrong. It was a mockery to call the United States of America the Land of the Free, if that included the freedom to starve quickly from lack of work or slowly from lack of money. He did not understand what was wrong, but if he got himself an education, he believed he might learn to understand.

At the jute mill he felt the need for a girl whom he could love and talk to. There were plenty of girls attracted to him as Mamie had been, but he wasn't interested in them. He knew what they were like, commonplace girls with only the thought of marriage and babies. They could not understand his desire for adventure and the company of men rougher than any they would dare to know, nor yet his passion for books and ideas far subtler than any they could appreciate.

He made friends with a blacksmith's apprentice called Louis Shattuck. Louis was a commonplace youth who was fond of fun with the girls. He thought Jack London was shy and backward, because he did not like the sort of girls who hung around waiting to be picked up and flirted with. He did not realize that Jack had already outgrown that with Mamie and others. What Jack wanted was a passion more romantic and of the spirit.

The nearest he approached to this was with a girl he met at a Salvation Army meeting. She wore a tam-o'-shanter and he fell in love with her. Her name was Haydee, he thought, though perhaps it was Heidi. He could not spell very well in those days, but his heart was ready for love.

They met perhaps a dozen times and exchanged perhaps a dozen kisses. It was a dumb passion. They said little, exchanged no ideas, and gave no promises. He never knew what she was really like. Something in her reached out to him as pure and simple and lovely. He always felt tender toward her, as someone who, after his bewilderment and sense that everything had been besmirched, restored for him the glory of innocence.

6. BIRTH OF A SOCIALIST

FLORA LONDON never told Jack about his real father. But she must have watched the growth in her son of qualities she had seen in W. H. Chaney. Chaney, for example, had spent many years at sea as a young man; Jack seemed to have inherited this love of the sea, and Chaney's love of reading, his inquisitive mind, and his refusal to accept that things should be, merely because they were. Was it possible that Jack also might have some ability to write?

One evening, when Jack came back from the jute mill, his mother showed him details of a literary competition in the San Francisco *Call*. The first prize was $25.00: a good night's haul for an oyster pirate or 250 hours working in the jute mill. It was something of a challenge to expect a young man working ten hours a day to write an article for a literary competition in his spare time. But Jack thought back to the voyage on the *Sophie Sutherland* and working in pencil on the corner of the kitchen table he produced *Typhoon off the Coast of Japan* in a couple of evenings and sent it off to the editor.

It won first prize, the second and third being awarded to university students. "The most striking thing," commented the judges, "is the largeness of grasp and steady force of expression that show the young artist."

Fired by his success, Jack sat down and wrote more. But there is a great difference between the standards used by judges in a literary competition and those of an editor receiving unsolicited contributions. Badly written and worse spelled, on cheap paper and in pencil, Jack London's stories and articles were rejected, for the most part without even being read. They looked unprofessional; and they were as unprofessional as they looked, a wild mixture of "literary" phrases and bad grammar through which the author's true originality only occasionally shone. The bright hope of becoming a writer faded.

Jack had been promised a raise in pay to twelve and a half cents an hour as soon as he had learned the work. But the promise wasn't kept, and Jack decided that there was no future in unskilled work. He would learn a trade, beginning at the bottom and rising to the top. Newspapers and magazines were full of the success stories of millionaires who had risen from nothing in the great Land of Opportunity.

Electrical engineering had a great future. So he went to the power plant of one of the Oakland street railways, and in an interview with the superintendent laid before him his plans for becoming an electrical engineer, starting at the bottom.

The superintendent listened to him with great sympathy. It wasn't everyone who came along wanting to start at the bottom, and the superintendent would be pleased to give him his chance. He could, in fact, begin work next morning, at seven o'clock; and his wages would be $30.00 a month, with one day off as holiday.

The pay was worse than he had received even in the cannery, as no overtime was paid. But Jack accepted this as the price he had to pay in order to learn electrical engineering.

The job consisted in passing coal to the furnace man. It was supposed to take him ten hours, but even working through his lunch hour he could not finish it in less than thirteen hours the first day. He was utterly exhausted by the work. The next day he managed to reduce the time slightly; and the day after slightly more. But he could not imagine how anyone had managed to cope with the work, until the fireman at last took him on one side and having sworn him to secrecy disclosed the fact that the work which Jack was doing had been done by two men, one working day and the other night shift and both receiving $40.00 a month. They had been sacked the day Jack came along with his offer to learn electrical engineering starting at the bottom. The fireman added that the superintendent had said that anyone telling Jack about the two men he had displaced would be given the sack and that he hadn't told him before, because he had been sure that Jack would collapse under the strain.

Instead of throwing his hand in then and there Jack continued to do the work of the two men, every day reducing his time until he had brought it down to ten hours. He hoped that the superintendent would see in his performance of this Herculean feat what a fine worker he had.

The superintendent was unimpressed, thinking probably that any lad working as hard as Jack for so little must be feeble-minded.

Then one morning the fireman showed Jack a cutting from a San Francisco newspaper. It was brief. It said that a coal passer with a wife and three children to support had killed himself because he couldn't find work.

"That's one of the guys whose job you're doing, kid," the fireman said.

That evening Jack left the electrical engineering business. He had not stayed long enough to injure himself permanently, but for a year afterward he had to wear wrist straps.

The effect of the work orgy in which he had indulged was to sicken him with work. He didn't care if he never settled down. Learning a trade could go hang. It was a whole lot better to royster and frolic over the world in the way he had previously done.

Jack London's life swung like a pendulum between responsibility and adventure, the call of civilization and the call of the wild. Flora and John London needed his wages as much as ever; but he was off again, following the blind urge of his destiny.

There was little or no work for unemployed men in Oakland and San Francisco. The same was true in many states of the Union. In Ohio so many men were out of work that an organizer called Coxey had started recruiting the unemployed into what he called The Army of the Commonwealth. His plan was that they should march on Washington and demand that Congress should vote $5,000,000 to be spent on giving the unemployed work on building roads.

"General" Coxey and his army were given so much notice in newspapers that the idea spread. In countless other cities contingents were organized to join up with Coxey's army in Washington. The organizer in Oakland was a man named Kelly. Kelly mobilized his unemployed into companies on military lines and arranged with the railroad authorities that they should be transported free in empty freight cars.

Jack persuaded a friend of his, Frank Davis, to go with him as a recruit in "General" Kelly's contingent. Most of the men who began the march with Kelly were serious, responsible people, who saw in the demonstration a chance of forcing the Government to admit that it was their business to see families did not starve for lack of work. But even though Jack London had just seen that a coal passer had killed himself because he had lost his job, he was still too young to understand what the march on Washington really meant. To him it was a lark. He didn't even trouble to find out when the army was starting from Oakland. When Frank Davis and he reached the freight yards, they found that the army had left eight hours before.

Frank Davis wanted to go back, but Jack wanted to show

him the tricks he'd learned with the road kids. He found a train ready to pull out, slid open a boxcar, told Frank to jump, and then climbed in behind him. Safe aboard, Jack told his friend how easy it would be to catch up with General Kelly, and he described all the things he knew about the road.

They left the boxcar, or "side-door Pullman," at Sacramento, only to find that Kelly's army had already left for Ogden. They jumped the Overland Express and rode as far as Truckee before they were chucked off, or "ditched."

Jack wasn't depressed. He was in his element. There was another Overland that night which they could catch. Frank caught it, but Jack, who'd waited to see his friend safely aboard, found it was going too fast. "Don't worry," he shouted, "I'll meet up with you some place."

Jack caught a freight train later. He was so tired by then that despite the cold he fell asleep and was sidetracked to Reno without waking up.

In Reno he found another contingent being formed to join the march on Washington. But he'd given his promise to Frank and it was better fun riding alone, anyway. So he did not wait for the marchers. He jumped a boxcar in which he rode for a day and a night. Landing at Wadsworth, he took shelter in an engine cab in the yards until he was turned out at four in the morning.

In the dawn he found an early freight going East. He rode the blind immediately behind the coal car, hoping to get some warmth from the engine. He got more than he wanted. When the train was traveling at forty miles an hour a spark from the engine landed in his overcoat pocket. He did not know that anything was wrong until his coat burst into flame. With one hand he hung on; with the other he beat out the fire. He put it out, but not before his overcoat and jacket were ruined. He had to throw them both away, but he caught up with Frank in Winnemukka.

When Jack told Frank about the contingent from Reno they decided to wait for its arrival and join it. Then a freight train came through and Jack persuaded Frank to jump aboard. Together they traveled East for another two days, and then Frank announced he wanted to go home. He couldn't stand the pace, the danger, the never knowing what would happen next, the strange mixture of people who formed the hobo world, the tricks and lies one had to master to dodge the bulls and persuade good people to part with food by telling just the right hard-luck story. Frank loathed the very things that gave Jack's life zest.

They parted company and Jack continued on his own, a

unit of the army marching on Washington but content to join up with others when the time came. In that journey East, thrown off trains at a moment's notice miles from anywhere, he learned how to approach a lonely farmstead, knowing that the story he told could mean the difference between having the dogs set on him and being invited into the kitchen for a square-sized meal. It was in that school he learned the importance of telling a good story; the better the story, the better the meal. Give rein to imagination and go hang with the truth!

In towns he tried the rich first. They could afford to give without feeling the pinch, and the food was better. But he knew that if he failed with the rich he would never go empty away from the poor. "A bone to the dog is not charity," he said later. "True charity is the bone shared with the dog when you are just as hungry as the dog."

Despite the hardship, and because of the danger, he enjoyed the contests with the train crews and bulls. It was a dangerous form of hide-and-seek with them trying to fling him off the moving train and him springing on again as nimbly. The memory of French Kid falling and the scream as he fell made him never forget just how dangerous it was.

He met up with the Reno detachment on the top of the Rocky Mountains in a blizzard. He dropped from the open blind where he was freezing and climbed into a boxcar where he found eighty-four men lying in two feet of straw, trying to keep warm.

For a day and a night they rode in the boxcar with nothing to eat or drink and the blizzard raging outside. To pass the time every man had to tell a story, a good story. Jack told his and listened to the others, entranced. Even in the stories which were failures he could see portraits of the men who told them.

They reached the plains of Nebraska, where they were fed

by sympathizers at Grand Island and then freighted through to Omaha. Up to that point, perhaps because there were empty wagons traveling from the Pacific Coast to the Middle West, the army had had a comparatively easy passage. In Omaha they were met by police at 1 A.M. They were turned out of the freight cars and marched down to the river under guard and shipped across to Council Bluffs. From there they were ordered to march in pouring rain to General Kelly's camp in a park five miles away.

Jack did not take orders easily, least of all from police. He and a Swede dodged out of their lines and looked for somewhere to sleep. The best place they could find was a saloon built on piles. Drenched to the skin, they slept on the floor with the wind whistling up through every crack in the floor boards, around from every crack in the sides, and down through every crack in the roof. Cold, wet, and sleepless, they rose at dawn and made their way out to General Kelly's camp.

From Omaha onward the railroad companies refused to provide boxcars. So General Kelly ordered his troops to march on foot. A dozen wagons were loaded with food and equipment given by sympathizers, and the army of the unemployed set forth, led by General Kelly astride a black horse.

Jack, always conspicuous in one way if not another, was in the rear file of the rear guard. After two days he had worn through the soles of his shoes, and he went to the commissary to ask for another pair. He was told there were none, so he took off what remained of his old shoes and walked barefoot until he was given a new pair.

The Army of the Commonwealth relied on the friendliness of the people in the towns and farmsteads through which they marched. Discipline was important to show that they were serious people in need of work, only asking to be allowed to live like decent, self-respecting human beings.

The least hint that they were hoodlums and tramps would set the good people of the countryside against them.

Jack London, a tramp at heart, hating discipline, was not a good marcher. He went along with the army while the going was good. At the first sign of its proving bad he deserted and begged enough money to buy himself a ticket on the railroad.

The army snowballed recruits as it went forward. By the time it reached Des Moines, numbers had risen to two thousand. Weary and footsore, they refused to march another step. They were housed in a deserted stove works and were fed six thousand meals a day, while the desperate city authorities tried to persuade the railroad companies to carry these unwelcome guests on the next stage of their journey.

The railroad companies refused. The authorities in Washington were alarmed at what they thought might be the beginning of a revolution, although all that Coxey was asking for was a program of public works such as President Franklin Delano Roosevelt initiated forty years later to meet a similar unemployment problem.

Kelly put his men on to building rafts on which to float down the Des Moines River. Meanwhile, promoting themselves from the rear of the rear guard to the van of the vanguard, Jack and nine other "hustlers" from his company acquired a boat of their own and went ahead. Traveling always twelve to twenty-four hours ahead of the main army, they would stop at some small riverside town and, hoisting the American flag, would ask to see what provision was being made for the army. Encouraged by the sight of so small a party, the farmers would bring out supplies from which Jack and his party would take their pick, leaving the rest for the nineteen hundred and ninety who were following.

Kelly's march was one of the first organized workers' demonstrations in American industrial history. Jack and his nine comrades could not have done more harm if they had been paid to wreck their efforts. Finding what was happening, Kelly sent a swift skiff down to overtake the "advance" boat; and when this failed, he sent two men on horseback to forewarn the farmers.

When Jack and his pals found that they were met with "the icy mitt," they fell back and rejoined Kelly's army. What is surprising is that they were allowed to do so. Jack still showed no signs of having learned discipline. He kept disappearing to work the tricks that he had learned from the road kids and in Quincy, Illinois, he begged enough clothes to reoutfit half his company.

The truth was that this Army of the Commonwealth was fired by no common ideal. Its ranks had been swelled by too many bums and hoboes, who had come along for the ride. By the time they reached Quincy, they had exhausted their good will. Newspaper stories of the thefts and swindlings in towns they had passed through had gone ahead of them, and their request for food was met with a blank refusal.

For a day and a half the men in Kelly's army starved. The point had been reached when they had to seize food or admit defeat.

Kelly refused to give the order to take the food they needed. He knew that the moment he did so he would be arrested on the charge of trying to overthrow the United States by force. And so his two thousand followers melted away even more quickly than they had snowballed while the progress was successful. He had only a handful of men with him by the time he reached Washington and was met by the news that General Coxey, who had started the whole thing, had been lodged in jail on a charge of walking on the grass!

Jack was not one of the remnant to reach Washington. He left the army at Quincy and made his way to Chicago, where a letter was waiting for him, containing $4.00 from Eliza. His mother's eldest sister, Mary Everhard, lived with her husband and two children on a farm near St. Joseph on Lake Michigan. Flora had suggested that Jack, who had never met any of his mother's relatives, should go to see them, if he found himself that way on his travels. Eliza did not want him to appear as a tramp. And so, with the $4.00, he bought shoes, a hat, a shirt, trousers, and an overcoat; and next day he crossed the lake to St. Joseph.

Jack must have been curious to meet his aunt Mary. His mother had told him a great deal about the history of the Wellman family, of which, despite her separation from it, she was proud. From his aunt Mary he probably tried to discover the secret of his own birth.[1]

Jack's purchases did not greatly impress his aunt Mary, who took him downtown and bought him a suit of clothes. But she was very drawn to the nephew she had never seen and gave "little parties for him, inviting those of his age or a little older." These parties of the gentle well-brought-up young people of St. Joseph must have been rather comic. But Jack got by with Aunt Mary.

Not so with his two boy cousins, Harry and Ernest Everhard; they disliked Jack as much as he disliked them. Jack had bought a notebook in which he wrote up notes of his trip across the States. This delighted Aunt Mary ("Jack's going to be a writer!") as much as it disgusted her two sons, who were hard at work haymaking. One afternoon, for example, when Ernest had cut and stacked the hay from a plot near the house, he called to Jack to help him with the loading. It was a hot day and there was the threat of a rainstorm which would ruin the hay.

Jack jumped to it and was pitching hay like an old hand

[1] It is unlikely that he succeeded. We don't know who gave him the name of Professor Chaney, but Jack did not write to ask him whether he was his father until he reached the age of twenty-one. It is possible that it took him all that time to find Chaney's address; but it is more probable that Jack was told about Chaney by John London when he felt that his own end was approaching.

when Aunt Mary caught sight of him and called, "Ernest, don't you know better than to expose Jack to that hot sun?"

Jack was made to stop work and go back to his writing under the shade of the trees, while Harry had to finish helping Ernest.

The two brothers, who had been regaled by Jack with stories about riding boxcars and crossing the desert under a sun that burned like an oven, were furious at their mother for taking him out of the mild heat of the Michigan sun. To them he told the tough side of his life; but to Aunt Mary he read stories which he was trying to write, crude, amateurish tales about knights and ladies, which Aunt Mary thought lovely.

Jack stayed for some weeks, savoring for the first time in his life the comforts of a solid, middle-class existence with plenty to eat and no worry about money.

But at last the urge came to be off again, first to Washington, D.C., where he diligently made a tour of United States Government buildings, ticking off each one in his notebook when he had "done" it. Leaving Washington in a blind on the Pennsylvania Express, he reached Baltimore, where he was chased by a "bull" through the yards and only got away by jumping another train—which he found took him back to Washington again. He was so angry that he wouldn't eat until he got back to Baltimore.

While he was bathing in the Susquehanna someone went through his clothing and stole his money and tobacco. It was all in the tramp's day, and later the same morning he cadged from a bunch of children what he could have sworn was some of the tobacco he had lost.

At last he reached New York City, astonished at the wealth and splendor and appalled by the poverty that existed side by side with it. In the morning he would "batter the main drag" for pennies and nickels. In the afternoons he would lie in the little park by City Hall, sheltering from the heat in the shade of a tree, drinking ice-cold milk at a penny a glass, and reading faulty copies of the latest books, which he bought cheap.

One afternoon he was watching a group of boys playing craps on the sidewalk. Suddenly one shouted "Chickey for the bulls!" and they disappeared like snow under boiling water. Jack, conscious of being innocent for once, strolled toward the park with his book under his arm. A policeman came over to him and without a word hit him over the head with his truncheon. Jack fell. The surprise and brutality of the attack dazed him. He wanted to protest his innocence. But wisdom prevailed. As he rose, he spurted off. It was better to act guilty than receive a sentence of thirty days for "resisting an officer."

He took to the road again, making for Niagara Falls. It was one of the Wonders of the World he was determined to see. He made for the Falls without troubling to buy any food. The immense cataracts falling and the huge clouds of uprising spray and the sunlight caught and broken in changing rainbows fascinated him. He watched all afternoon, and as the sun went down and night fell and the moon rose, he could not tear himself away from this glory, always marvelous but from one moment to another different. He did not leave the Falls until eleven at night, and then he climbed a fence and found a field in which to sleep.

He awoke at dawn. He was eager to see what the Falls would look like in the first light. He hurried down the quiet, sleeping street and saw three men coming toward him. He could not see who they were until it was too late. The one in the middle was a constable, those on either side were hoboes.

"Where you staying, kid?" shouted the constable.

"No place," Jack said.

"Then come alonga me."

Before he knew what was happening, he was arrested and taken to Niagara Falls jail.

"Why?"

"Staying no place," said the constable. "You're a vagrant."

New York State needed cheap labor, and the easiest way to recruit it was to arrest men for vagrancy—even though thousands of men had marched on Washington to ask for just such work.

Later the same morning Jack and fifteen others were taken before the judge. The state of New York was running the law on a shoestring as well, and the judge had to act as his own clerk of the court. As clerk of the court, he called out the name of the offender and the charge. As judge, he sentenced the offender to thirty days' hard labor; and as clerk of the court, he wrote down the sentence.

People are liable to complain of the slow process of the law. But in no time Jack and the fifteen others were sentenced. Each pair of prisoners was handcuffed, Jack to a tall Negro, and then a chain was passed over the eight pairs of handcuffs and the sentenced men were marched down to the railroad station to be put aboard a train to Erie County Penitentiary.

This experience did not increase Jack London's respect for the law, although it was never very high. But it increased his sympathy with outcasts who for one reason or another had fallen foul of the law. On the train he made friends with an old lag who had been in and out of so many prisons that he knew all the ropes. By the time he had reached the penitentiary he had made a friend who would stand him in good stead.

At the penitentiary their heads were shaved. They were dressed in prison stripes. And next morning they were put to the work which was the reason for their arrest—unloading canal boats. The work was backbreaking and the food appalling, bread and water with meat only once a week, and that boiled so long that all the goodness had gone from it.

Jack's friend soon found his feet. He had friends among the "trusties," the convicts who were given prison jobs because they could be trusted not to escape. After a couple of days he wangled for himself and Jack the cushy job of "hall men," serving out bread and water and keeping order. Just as when he was a newsboy he had built up a trade starting with cigarette cards, so in the penitentiary he bartered extra bits of bread for books and tobacco and swapped safety pins for extra meat.

As a hall man Jack saw more of what went on in the pen than if he had been unloading canal barges. The law seemed to him a solemn name for cruelty and injustice. He saw men go mad. He watched epileptics falling in fits. He witnessed a prisoner flogged down a flight of stone steps. He heard another beaten to death. Here hell was not hereafter, but on earth; and not far from the wonder of Niagara Falls.

Yet the world inside the penitentiary was not so very different from the world outside. He saw the humanity of the convicts, the trusties, and the guards. In the pen human nature was no better than it was on the Oakland water front, in the fo'c's'le of the *Sophie Sutherland,* the jute mill, or the freight yards. But it was very little worse.

The only thing that embarrassed him was the friendship of the old lag. His friend had decided that in Jack he had found a perfect partner. Jack listened to his career of crime, the cribs he'd cracked, the joints he'd cased, with a calm mind. But he was disturbed by his friend's assumption that when they were released they were going into partnership together.

They were released together after thirty days. Jack did not like to tell his friend that he had no intention of embarking on a career of crime. He went with him to Buffalo and had a drink in a saloon, where Jack excused himself and ran all the way to the freight yards and jumped the first train heading West.

It took him many weeks riding the Canadian railroads to reach Vancouver on the Pacific three thousand miles away. He was never again arrested for vagrancy, although he had many narrow escapes. But on that journey back he was a very different young man from the undisciplined road kid who had started out in pursuit of General Kelly's army.

In that army, if he had chosen to listen, there were plenty of Socialists, who had read the gentle words of William Morris or the fiercer works of Karl Marx. But he wasn't ready to listen.

On the way home, in boxcars and hoboes' camps, he heard the same talk, and now it made sense to him. Campfire professors told him about the war of the classes, the inevitable struggle between the rich and the poor, in which the rich would get richer and richer and the poor poorer and poorer, and he remembered the way his own wages, when he worked inside the law, had got lower and lower the more he had tried to rise.

By the time he reached Vancouver the wild boy who had left Oakland had become a dedicated Socialist. He believed his task in the world was to overthrow the Constitution of the United States, in the way General Kelly had failed to do at Quincy.

But before he did so, he had to get home and study. High school and university called. It was a very serious revolutionary who signed on the *Umatilla* at Vancouver as a sailor making for San Francisco.

If he had a dream, it was of becoming the first Socialist President of the United States.

7. READING "THE BOOKS"

WHEN JACK returned to Oakland, having followed his blind destiny across the United States and back through Canada, he knew that he had to get himself a higher education. He was through with manual labor. He would never again try to earn a living by selling his brawn. He had brains and he would sell them, whether it was by writing or as a politician. For both these careers he had a wealth of experience unique in a young man of nineteen. He had been a pirate, a fish patrolman, a canner, a jute-mill hand, an able-bodied seaman, a coal passer, a road kid, a tramp, and a convict. He had seen far more of the seamy side of life than most respectable American citizens saw in their lifetimes.

But he could not make use of this experience, even properly digest it, without further education. His speech was appalling. He not only said "I ain't done nothin'," but also did not know that there was anything wrong in saying it. He knew little of the rules of grammar or syntax. He had accumulated a number of words from books he had read, but he did not know how to pronounce them correctly or exactly what their meanings were. Before learning to think he had to build up a vocabulary to think with.

He had done with the books of travels and voyages. What he needed now were grammars and dictionaries to show him how to write correctly, and books of political, social, and economic theory to explain the reasons for what he had found out for himself: why the rich should become richer and the poor always poorer, why in a country abounding with wealth there should be so many men without jobs.

Luckily Jack found the family less destitute than usual. John London was in work for the time being and Eliza had been able to help her father and Flora out of what she had saved from her housekeeping. Ida had married Frank Miller. So now there were only the two old people.

There was a family conference about Jack's education. Jack was nineteen and in a way it was a terrible humiliation for him to have to go back to high school and learn with boys and girls of fifteen who were better than he was at things such as algebra and knew how to talk and behave more decently. But he was willing to try it and Eliza promised money to help him buy his books. On the strength of the prize he had won from the San Francisco *Call* and the stories he was writing the family believed in him enough to stake him.

The only thing that Jack liked about the high school was the school magazine, which accepted his stories and articles for every issue. Like every other young writer, he learned a great deal from reading his own work in print. What had seemed so wonderful in his own handwriting was revealed in all its faults the moment it appeared in cold print. He learned more from reading his printed stuff than any high-school English master could teach him. A professional writer could perhaps have taught him more still, but he knew no professional writers.

Jack would have been prepared to accept the humiliation of sitting in class with a lot of kids if he hadn't found that he was being kept back to their speed. He was always a fast learner and, with his maturer brain, he found that most of the time he was kicking his heels. In age he was ready to enter a university now, but at high school it would be another three years before he could enter.

There was another family conference. Jack had found a crammer who claimed to be able to cover the three-year high-school course in two years. Eliza promised to provide the fees.

Jack went to the crammer and applied himself with that terrific concentration that he brought to everything, including passing coal. He set himself not to learn, but to learn how to learn, to evolve a method of study. After five weeks the crammer gave him his money back. At the rate he was going, the crammer said, Jack would have finished the two-year course in four months. It would never do if the university authorities found out that he took two years to teach a course that could be learned in a sixth of that time.

So Jack went on his lonely way. He had already learned how to learn. He plunged ahead, finding it all the easier to go at his own breakneck speed, because he was sure what he needed to learn.

At the same time as he was studying the subjects which he needed to qualify him for the university he devoured the book of the philosophers and economists who were in vogue at that time: Herbert Spencer, Fourier, Fiske, Nietzsche, and Karl Marx, all of whom disagreed with one another in everything except the conviction that man, by the cultivation of reason, could control his future.

He became convinced that socialism would cure the ills of society. What was wrong was the capitalist system and not the weakness of human nature. He and John London and Flora, he decided, were the victims of this system.

It was, of course, partly true. But the reason why John and Flora had found themselves on the rocks over and over again was not the fault of the capitalist system. It was that as soon as John London started on a sound venture, Flora wrecked it with her greed for making money quickly and her absurd reliance on spirit guidance for the choice of lottery tickets and investments. And the reason why he himself when he started to make good money as an oyster pirate saved nothing for his education or his family had also nothing to do with the system. He had spent the money in saloons. All through his life he was to draw the wrong conclusion. He never saw a situation as a whole. He dashed from one side to the other. Either hoard money or fling it away. Never steer a middle course.

Once Jack London had decided that all that was wrong in his life could be blamed on the capitalist system and could be cured through the miracle of socialism he flung himself into the movement with the passion of his simple spirit. He joined a debating society in Oakland called the Henry Clay Society, after the American statesman who was a champion of the abolition of slavery. The Henry Clay Society in Oakland was a meeting place for comfortable middle-class intellectuals, teachers, students, doctors, lawyers, and economists. They liked to meet sociably and discuss in a gentle, earnest, civilized way the future of the United States (and sometimes the rest of the world).

Jack London irrupted into the Henry Clay Society like a fighting bull into a tea party. The gentle members were used to discussing social conditions. But when Jack London stood up, broad, husky, and incredibly good-looking (apart from his teeth, which were ruined by decay and chewing tobacco to kill the pain in the exposed nerves), he electrified them because he was talking about things which he really knew. They talked about prison conditions. He had been in prison. They talked about sweated labor. His labor had been sweated. They talked about unemployment. He had been out of work and marched with General Kelly. They talked about "social conditions." He got up and spoke to them, like a machine gun spitting bullets. And there he was, in the flesh, the living embodiment of the social conditions they were talking about.

He started talking at the Henry Clay while he was at high school. For a time there was the fantastic situation of his double life. Fifteen-year-old Mary X would come home from high school and talk about this awful roughneck, Jack London, who chewed tobacco, went down to the water front and drank in Johnny Heinhold's Last Chance, who didn't know his Pythagoras Theorem, but knew every oath under the sun. And there was Mr. X, her father, who had listened the night

before to Jack talking about prison conditions, who hailed Jack London as a wonderful speaker, a dynamic force in American politics, and so on.

The closest friend Jack made in the Henry Clay Society was Edward Applegarth, the same age as Jack but already a student at Berkeley University. Edward came of an English family. He had a good mind and a keener wit than most of his fellow undergraduates. He admired Jack for his strength, his vigor of speech, and his originality of mind. And Jack admired Edward because of the ease with which he took for granted all the things which he, Jack, had come by the hard way. Edward had the background that Jack would have loved to have.

Edward took Jack home to meet his parents and his sister Mabel, who was three years older. Jack had never been in a house like the Applegarths'. It was like a palace. There were real oil paintings on the walls and no holes in the carpets, and there was enough food to have a second helping if you wanted to. He wanted to have a second helping, but he never did, because he wanted to hide the fact that at his home there wasn't even enough for a decent first helping. Also there were books, the poems of Longfellow, Swinburne, and Tennyson; and a piano at which Mabel Applegarth played. Mabel Applegarth played and sang in a voice which, though not powerful, was very moving. She had golden hair and blue eyes and her speaking voice was beautiful, especially when she read poetry. Jack called her the Lily Maid.

She knew all about poetry because she had been reading English literature for three years at the University of Berkeley. The moment Jack saw her he fell head over heels in love with her.

She asked him to come to see them again, and he went through agonies, trying to decide whether she meant it, and if so, how soon was "again." He went to the public library and took out a book on social etiquette in order to learn about what to do with his hat and which knives, forks, and spoons were used for what.

Mabel Applegarth, fragile, delicate, and refined, took a pleasure in taking this husky, handsome young man in hand, in teaching him how to speak properly, correcting his grammar and pronunciation, telling him what words were not permissible in polite society, and seeing that his fingernails were trimmed and clean. Jack was so much in love that her correction became a form of bliss, although he would have resented it from anybody else. The only other girl whom he had regarded with equal reverence had been Haydee. Mabel was far superior, because she was "a lady," familiar with all the refinements of gracious living, literature, music, good food, solid furniture, and pretty clothes. These stood for spiritual qualities that were lacking in Mamie and other girls he had known.

He slaved at his work and entered the university, paying his way by doing odd jobs, such as mowing lawns. At the same time he continued with his writing—articles, stories, poems, which he showed to Mabel for her comments. He had abandoned the romantic vein that had pleased his aunt Mary for realistic stories about the sort of life he knew. Mabel read them and pointed out his mistakes in grammar and spelling or the misuse of words.

"I don't care about that," he would say impatiently. "What do you think of the thing as a whole, what I'm driving at?"

Mabel, unfortunately, did not think much. There were so many beautiful things in life to write about that she could not understand his concentration on what was nasty. Longfellow did not write about what was nasty, nor did Tennyson; and they were really great, weren't they?

Jack tried to explain to her that he was trying to find the meaning of life as he had seen it. In that life there was much that was violent and savage and foul, but if he could find out the meaning of it, he could make it beautiful. Mabel shook her head. That wasn't the way they taught her about English literature at the University of Berkeley.

At the university, as at the crammer's, Jack set himself to learn the method of learning. By the time his money ran out once more he felt that he had mastered the university method. He knew enough to be able to teach himself in future. He was able to think, and that was something more important to get from a university than a degree.

While he was still at the university, his political activities brought him notoriety. The Applegarths and their well-to-do friends were not the only people to be impressed by Jack London's speeches in the Henry Clay Society. Radicals and Socialists saw him as a valuable recruit to their cause. He had a good forthright mind, wide experience for his age, a marvelous face and body, and an Irishman's gift of gab. They enlisted him in the newly founded Socialist party of Oakland and began to groom him as a speaker. He was asked to speak at the small meetings in workers' halls and at larger open-air demonstrations. At one of these in City Hall Park he denounced the capitalist system with all the passion of his simple eloquence. Ten minutes later he was under arrest and within the hour he was in jail, charged this time, not with vagrancy, but with incitement to overthrow the United States Constitution.

Next day he hit the Oakland headlines as "The Boy Socialist." Solid businessmen and members of the Chamber of Commerce clamored for him to receive a prison sentence. But the judge let him off with a warning, in view of his youth, that a second offence would be punished severely.

The Socialist local hailed Jack as a hero; but many of his respectable acquaintances in the Henry Clay Society turned their backs on him. He had become a controversial figure, to whom the young intellectuals in Oakland gave allegiance. Edward Applegarth approved; his sister Mabel considered, like the judge, that the first offence might be pardoned, but it was not to be repeated.

Edward stood by Jack in another, more personal matter. Jack had discovered the name and address of Professor Chaney and wrote to ask him whether it was true that he was his father. Jack confided the secret to Edward and asked if he might use the Applegarths' address instead of his mother's, for Chaney to send his reply to.

Jack wrote several times before he received an answer. Even then his curiosity was not satisfied. Chaney admitted that he had known Flora Wellman and loved her. But he denied that she had ever had a son by him. The old man, one feels, was sorry for Jack but was not prepared to saddle himself with a son. He had married someone else and did not want to upset his wife by acknowledging he was Jack's father.

So Jack London was left with the mystery of his birth, a mystery which haunted him in moments of depression, but from which he was to escape when he was able to play the part of Prince among Men.

After leaving the university Jack tried again to repeat the success he had had with *Typhoon off the Coast of Japan.* He locked himself in his room and for fifteen hours a day he wrote poems, essays, tracts, and short stories. One of his troubles was that California, one of the last states in the Union to be Americanized, had little literary activity. Most of the magazines were published in the East, in New York City, Boston, and Chicago. Jack bombarded them with manuscripts, which were rejected by return of post. Money that was sorely needed for buying food and paying rent went for postage, and there was nothing to show in return.

Jack's second assault on the literary world had failed even more dismally than the first. Acknowledging himself beaten for the time being, he took a job in a school laundry, with a wage of $30.00 a month, plus board and lodging. Deducting what he needed for tobacco and cigarette papers, he sent the rest to his mother. At least, he thought, he would have some time to read and perhaps write a little.

He never read or wrote a word. He was back in the treadmill again, sorting, washing, starching, and ironing six days a week, too tired at night to write or read. On Sunday he would bicycle to see Mabel, who did not seem so upset as he was at the failure to achieve publication. It merely proved that she was right. What editors wanted, she had always maintained, were nice stories about nice people. Besides, writing was a very risky occupation. If only he had a nice, steady job, she said, then he could write in his spare time.

The job in the laundry could not last. He was certain to break out as he had done after his bondage in the cannery and again after the jute mill and the powerhouse. The first had driven him to join the oyster pirates, the second to enlist in the Army of the Commonwealth. This time it was the lure of gold in the far Klondike.

The newspapers were filled with wild stories of fabulous gold strikes in the Yukon, the far northwest of Canada. Every mining prospector in the continent who could raise a grubstake hurried North; and soon the gold fever spread through the population of Canada and the United States in general. Doctors, lawyers, tradesmen, and others suddenly threw up their jobs and joined the mad rush North.

Eliza Shepard's husband caught the fever, though in his sixties he should have known better. Eliza raised $1,500 to finance her husband and Jack, and on March 12, 1897, they set sail on the *Umatilla* (the same ship on which Jack had worked his passage back from Vancouver to San Francisco). With them they took fur clothes for the Arctic, camping kit, runners, thongs, and tools, plus the thousand pounds of food per head which the Canadian Government demanded of all prospectors entering the territory.

Of how Mabel took Jack's departure there is no record, but Mrs. Applegarth probably expressed the view of the whole family when she wrote:

> Dear John,
>
> We have just received your letter with the awful news that you are about to start for Alaska. Oh, dear John, do be persuaded to give up the idea, for we feel certain that you are going to meet your death, and we shall never see you again. What your object may be we cannot even think, but we feel as though we shall never see you again. John, do give up the thought, for you will never come back again, never. Your father and mother must be nearly crazed over it. Now, even at the eleventh hour, dear John, do change your mind and stay. With lots of love to all, and hoping to hear better news, I remain your sincere friend . . . .

John London was far from being crazed over it. He said good-by to Jack from what proved several months later to be his deathbed. He begged Jack to take him along. "If you could only get me up there in the snows, Jack, I'd get strong right off." He had great belief in the Klondike trip and kept saying after Jack left, "He'll come out all right. You watch his smoke. And come out big, mark my words."

8. THE GOLD RUSH

FOR YEARS men had been prospecting for gold through Yukon and Alaska in the far northwest of the American continent. Strikes of alluvial gold had been made in large enough quantities to encourage prospectors to spend their whole lives in the search for a sudden fortune.

But nothing which these hardened old experts found compared to the strike made by a complete amateur in August 1896. This first great strike was made in Rabbit Creek, a tributary running into the Klondike River, a place where it was so unlikely to find gold that none of the experts had ever troubled to pan it. The Bonanza strike in Rabbit Creek and the Eldorado, found soon after up a river running into Rabbit Creek, were the richest finds of alluvial gold that had ever been discovered in North America.

It was not till nearly a year later that Jack London and Captain Shepard set sail; and in the meantime men from all over Canada and the United States and even from Europe and farther afield had been seized by the gold fever, flung up their jobs, and journeyed thousands of miles toward the Klondike. It was the invasion of one of the most desolate and barren areas on earth by enough gold-hungry men to make up a small army. But these men were not disciplined like an army. They were all engaged in a race against time, to reach at least Dawson City, at the junction of the Klondike and Yukon rivers, before the early winter clamped down. But they were also engaged in a race against one another, each rushing to be ahead to stake his claim.

Jack knew that old Captain Shepard and he had little chance of winning through on their own. There were two routes to the Klondike, one through northern Alaska up the Yukon River and the other involving the long climb from Dyea Beach over the mountains through the Chilkoot Pass and then proceeding downstream through lakes and along rivers to Dawson.

Even if they had had enough money to pay their steamer fares up the Yukon, all places were booked ahead until the freeze-up. The southern route from Dyea kept open longer, but Jack realized that their best chance of winning through would be to make up a team. He was confident that he could handle the navigation, given a boat. And on board the *Umatilla* he made friends with a little man called Merritt Sloper, who had been a carpenter by trade and had had some experience with boats. Between them they could manage the part of the journey that lay by water. For his other two partners he chose husky great men, Jim Goodman, who had been a miner, and Fred Thompson, who seemed to have some experience of prospecting. The only member of the team who seemed to have no contribution to make was Captain Shepard.

When the *Umatilla* left San Francisco they had been told that the price they would have to pay Indian porters for carrying their gear across the Chilkoot Pass would be six cents a pound. But by the time they reached Dyea Beach the price had already risen to thirty cents a pound, and even as they stood there, aghast at this blow to their calculations, the price soared first to forty and then fifty cents a pound.

They were caught. Dyea was in Alaska, the Klondike was in the Canadian state of Yukon. When they crossed the Alaskan-Yukon frontier at Lake Marsh each man had to produce $500 cash and 1,000 pounds of food. If they left their food behind, they would be interned and sent back for lack of food. If they paid for it to be portered, they would be sent back for lack of money. There was nothing for it but to do their own portering. Poor old Captain Shepard went as far as the beginning of the trail, took one look at the wicked trail winding up the mountain, and confessed himself beaten. He went back on the same boat that had brought him.

The other four set to work as fast as they could. It was already early August and even without the burden of Shepard it was going to be a struggle to beat the winter, doing their own portering.

From the sea the trail wound three miles up to the head of the Chilkoot Pass, described in the picturesque language of the gold rush as "the worst trail this side of hell." It was a foot track used up till then by a few dozen Indians and trappers. Now hundreds of heavily laden men were staggering up the loose shale into mud and slush and, at the higher levels, snow.

Jack and his three partners were soft and out of condition after the voyage. But that climb to the top of the pass soon brought them into training. Between them they had more than 5,000 pounds' weight of food and gear. A man's load was 150 pounds; and they made four journeys a day to the

---

See map opposite. Jack London arrived at Dyea in the summer of 1898 by steamship. His party traveled fifteen miles upriver by canoe; they carried their gear over the mountains and through swamps to Lake Lindeman.

There they built a boat and sailed down the Lewes River to the winter camp. They struck gold there—as they thought—and sailed down to Dawson to register the claim. Finding their mistake, they sailed back to camp; and in the break-up next spring, Jack London floated down to Dawson by raft.

He went to the hospital with scurvy and later took the river steamer down the Yukon to Hamilton, where he shipped for home.

SIBERIA
Arctic Ocean
Hamilton
Yukon R.
Yukon R.
Fort Yukon
CANADA
Dawson
Klondike R.
Klondike City
YUKON
Winter Camp
ALASKA
(U.S.A.)
Bering Sea
Lewes R.
Rapids
Gulf of Alaska
Lindeman
Chilkoot Pass
Dyea
Coast Mountains
Sitka
0
100
200
300
400
MILES

head of the pass, caching their stuff at the top and then going back for more. With porters they could have done it in a morning and arrived fresh. It took the four of them two and a half days; and then there lay ahead of them a further twenty-two miles of porterage between the top of the pass and Lake Lindeman, the start of their passage downstream.

The scenes on this journey stamped themselves on Jack London's memory. Some he merely used as anecdotes; as for example, the tale of the man on the climb to the top of the pass who was so tired that he sat down on a fallen tree to regain his breath. The weight of his pack was so great that it toppled him over backward headfirst into a deep snowdrift. He couldn't call out, but as Jack London plodded up the trail he caught sight of something out of the tail of his eye. It was a pair of legs waving in the air. Very cautiously Jack rested his own pack on the log to prevent himself falling back in the same way as the man had done. Then he eased the pack off his shoulders and pulled the man out by the legs.

But there were other scenes: of the desperate struggle of men, too old for such a journey, who had not had the courage to admit that they were beaten, as Captain Shepard had, and who were caught on the mountain, too weak to go on and too weak to go back.

That first ordeal, the climb to the pass, was the most grueling. But the twenty-two miles that followed, though gradually downhill, was as great a strain. There were swift, ice-cold streams across which there were no bridges or ferries. In what some wit had nicknamed "Pleasant Valley" there was a swamp through which they had to wade, the weight of their packs driving them up to the knees in freezing ooze and muck. What made the journey so heartbreaking was that most stages had to be made over and over again to bring the full loads of food and gear along. Now and again there was a lake across which some unsuccessful prospector was running a ferry, preferring the certainty of making money out of helping others to reach the Klondike to the risk of finding nothing if he went there himself. Jack and his team used all the ferryboats they could, leaving little Sloper to book their passages and guard the gear while they brought up what was left in the rear.

But there were other lakes, across which there was no ferry, and these they had to walk around in one of the longest, maddest obstacle races in the history of man.

They reached Lake Lindeman at last and found a great crowd waiting there, fighting for places on the boats plying ferry.

This was the moment that Jack and Merritt Sloper and the others had planned for in advance. Leaving Fred Thompson to look after their food and gear, the other three beat up the side of the lake until they found a good stand of timber. Jack had sketched the flat-bottomed craft they needed, Sloper had worked out what this meant in terms of planks and joining. Together they felled the trees, whipsawed the planks, and while Sloper and Goodman built the boat, the *Yukon Belle,* Jack sewed the sails.

The race was to the swift, and on their tails was the winter, to say nothing of hundreds of others desperate for the gold of the Klondike.

In surprisingly quick time the *Yukon Belle* was finished and Jack had completed his own part of the job far enough ahead of the other two to have time to compose a poem in honor of his craft, probably the only poem that was ever written to a boat in the gold rush. They sailed down, picked up Thompson and the cargo, and beat it across the lake, under sail when the wind was right but otherwise pulling at the oars.

Jack loved to talk about this trip later in his life. And the more he talked about it, the more exciting it became. His motto was: "Make it vivid. Truth doesn't matter so much, so long as it lives." And the versions he left of it became so vivid that they are very difficult to believe. It became a flight from the advance of winter. Lakes froze behind them as they sped downstream. They were pursued by ice. They would look back on the water through which they had sailed and see it setting hard in their wake!

Yet they were making steadily north into country to which the winter had come earlier. Vividness had got the better of truth. The winter was not closing in behind them, and it did not close in in front of them.

When they reached the Alaskan-Yukon frontier at Lake Marsh they found a pile-up of gold-rushers who had been daunted by the rapids. These rapids were in two stages, with a break in the middle. After the first rapid the river broadened out in a great whirlpool, and then they plunged again into a lower rapid.

Some of the gold-rushers had tried to ride the rapids, but they had all failed. There was a sense of tragedy about the men who had reached the frontier. They had passed the frontier barrier only to be faced by something far more dangerous. For the first time they realized that instead of finding gold they might lose their lives. Some of them tried to porter their stuff and their boats below the rapids, an appalling task involving days of dragging, lugging, and hauling. Others stayed at the head of the rapids, unsure whether to go on or to go back.

Jack was in his element here. They tied up the *Yukon Belle* and walked down the rapids, with Jack looking over the hidden hazards from above. He must have won the confidence of his partners, because when he told them they could ride the rapids, they put their lives in his hands.

The people who had been drowned trying to shoot the

rapids had tried to steer their way against the water. Jack's theory was that they should use the current to carry them through. They began the passage with Merritt Sloper rowing and Jack steering with an oar in the stern. But as soon as they entered the rapids, Jack yelled to Merritt Sloper to ship his oars, and he carried them through to the river below in a couple of minutes.

One can imagine the effect this must have had on the people struggling to get their gear along the riverbank to see the *Yukon Belle* shoot past them ahead on the race to the claims.

Jack had promised that if he succeeded he would come back and help a Mr. Ret and his wife to take their boat through. He was besieged with offers from other people but he would not accept them. But he risked his own life and Sloper's a second time because he felt it so gallant that a woman should dare to make this journey with her husband.

They went downriver until on October 9 they reached an old encampment on Upper Island on the Henderson River. There were many people in different abandoned fur traders' huts there, prepared to stay out the winter. It was eighty miles from Dawson City and even farther from Rabbit Creek. But this was the country of Henderson, the man who discovered Rabbit Creek.

Jack had read all that there was to read about the new gold strikes. He knew that gold was where you least expected to find it. They decided to lay up in one of the cabins and try their luck panning up some of the side streams which were not yet frozen. On October 12, in Henderson Creek, Fred Thompson discovered sand rich in gleaming grains. The yield was very high, and as they staked out their claim, Fred Thompson reckoned that it should net them each at least a quarter of a million dollars. For three days they surveyed the whole area, saying nothing to the other men on the island. Early on the fourth day, leaving most of their provisions and their gear behind, they took the *Yukon Belle* and dropped down to Dawson City with a bag of dust to be assayed and a map of the area in which they wanted to register the claims they had staked.

In high excitement they hurried from the mooring stage to the assayer's office in the busy little boom town. Until the claim was actually registered, they feared that somehow or other they would be cheated of their fortune.

And they were right. The assayer opened the bag and looked at the brightly gleaming dust, and then he grinned. "Ain't you never seen mica?" he asked.

The bottom had fallen out of their world. It no longer seemed important to hurry back to Upper Island and get in as much work as possible before the winter closed completely in. Dawson City with its saloons and dance halls and its wild tales of fortunes made and lost held them for the next seven weeks. All of them felt they needed some form of relaxation after the months of hardship fighting their way in; and to Jack with his love of company, the people whom he met and listened to were to prove as rich a strike as the gold dust Fred Thompson had imagined he had discovered in Henderson Creek.

Finally, on December 3, their money spent, the four partners left Dawson City and reached Upper Island four days later.

The log cabins on Upper Island were a group which had been built years before by fur traders from the Bering Sea and then abandoned. There were about seventy other men wintering there, and as it was on a main route, people of all sorts: Indians, half-breeds, trappers, and prospectors, called in on their way through.

In a cabin close to Jack's was an older man, called Hargrave, from Colfax, Washington, who wrote a description of the first time he went to Jack's cabin.

"London was seated on the edge of a bunk, rolling a cigarette. He smoked incessantly. One of his partners, Goodman, was preparing a meal, and the other, Sloper, was doing some carpentry work. From the few words which I overheard as I entered I surmised that Jack had challenged some of Goodman's orthodox views, and that the latter was doggedly defending himself in an unequal contest of wits. Many times afterward I myself felt the rapier thrust of London's, and knew how to sympathize with Goodman.

"Jack interrupted the conversation to welcome me, and his hospitality was so cordial, his smile so genial, his good-fellowship so real, that it instantly dispelled all reserve. I was invited to participate in the discussion, which I did, much to my subsequent discomfiture.

"That day has become consecrated in my memory. During the course of my life I have met men who were worth while; but Jack was the one man with whom I have come in personal contact who possessed the qualities of heart and mind that made him one of the world's geniuses."

Hargrave was an older man than Jack (though Jack nicknamed him "Kid"). His partners were Judge Sullivan and Dr. Harvey, both men of considerable education. Among them and Jack and whoever else was around there were interminable discussions about evolution, religion, socialism —all the questions which divided the world outside but which might be thought unimportant to men held up in their search for gold by the Arctic winter.

Jack used to provoke these discussions, which stimulated him quite as much as physical daring. Thought was an adventure of the mind, an intellectual sport in which he delighted to win.

Hargrave, Judge Sullivan, and Dr. Harvey were the sort of

people he had met in the Henry Clay Society. Far more important were the old prospectors, the fur trappers, the "squaw men" (that is, white men married to Indian women), the half-breeds, and the Indians.

"Everything interested him," wrote Hargrave, "events, things, men—all kinds and manner of men. To the others a native was a 'siwash,' but Jack would talk to them, in so far as his limited command of Chinook and their even more restricted command of English would permit. He would entertain them and invite them into the cabin, and I believe that he learned more about them, their customs, their primitive souls, than was known to the oldest sourdough squaw man on the river."

Jack was "irrationally generous," in Hargrave's words; and his generosity to all and sundry, including the natives, began to tell on the nerves of his three partners. Flour cost $120 a sack; and it was their flour and beans and bacon as much as his own that Jack was so generous in dishing out.

As the winter crept on, the atmosphere among the four men—who in the first place had been drawn together only because they made a good team to win as far as they had done—became more and more tense. It was brought to a head when Jack by mistake ruined the cutting edge of Sloper's favorite ax.

Jack changed his cabin and moved in as Dr. Harvey's partner. Hargrave teamed up with the judge, and the four of them lived together until the spring came.

The lack of fresh food began to tell on them. This was long before the discovery of vitamin deficiency or the manufacture of vitamin pills. Hargrave was the first to go down with scurvy, because of lack of fresh fruit or vegetables containing vitamin C. Jack and Harvey went out in search of fresh meat, which they thought would cure the scurvy. They traveled eighty miles each way to bring in a moose. But it did not help Hargrave, who had to be taken downriver to Dawson on a sled.

Before the spring thaw Jack himself had scurvy; yet despite his failing strength Jack helped Dr. Harvey dismantle the cabin in which they had been sleeping, make a raft from the logs, and float it down to Dawson.

There they sold it to the sawmill for several hundred dollars. But Jack was too ill to go on. He was taken to the hospital, where they told him that the only cure for his complaint was to get back to a country of fresh food.

On Tuesday, June 8, 1898, he began the voyage for the outside, down the Yukon in a frail open boat through mush ice, keeping at the same time a log of the voyage which showed that having resigned the hopes of finding gold he was at last turning his thoughts back to writing. Even then he was merely thinking of writing for *Outing Magazine* and *The Youth's Companion* about the country through which they passed in the three-week trip. The only reference in the course of the whole voyage to his physical condition, which must have been agonizing, was: "Given some fresh potatoes and a can of tomatoes for my scurvy, which has now almost crippled me from my waist down. Right leg drawing up; can no longer straighten it; even in walking must put my whole weight on toes. These few raw potatoes and tomatoes are worth more to me at the present stage of the game than an Eldorado claim. What wots it, though a man gain illimitable wealth and lose his own life?"

That was to be horribly prophetic.

9. POSTMAN OR WRITER?

GIVEN FRESH fruit and vegetables, Jack soon recovered from his scurvy. But when he finally reached Oakland he found his mother's finances in a very unhealthy condition. She was living in a tiny cottage, with Johnny Miller, her stepdaughter Ida's boy, whom she had practically adopted. Her credit was stretched to the full and there was a host of small debts incurred by John London before his death which Jack felt in duty bound to settle.

Jack himself had no money. He registered at five employment bureaus, scanned the advertisement columns of all the daily newspapers, applied for work as a studio model. But there was even less work for a young unskilled laborer of twenty-two than there had been for unskilled boys, when Jack left school nine years before. Many jobs were closed to him, because Jack London, though he was a Socialist and a stanch believer—he said—in organized labor, did not hold any union membership card.

He sat for the Civil Service examinations for postmen and passed with the top score. But as there were no vacancies at the moment, he passed the time with small casual jobs and writing. He wrote an article *Down the River*, based on the notes he had taken during his trip down the Yukon. He sent it to a San Francisco paper and it was returned. He had concentrated on giving a lot of undigested information, instead of giving it a dramatic theme, linked, for example, to the gold rush or to his own attack of scurvy.

Then he tried a 20,000-word serial especially for *The*

Youth's Companion, which he finished and typed in a week. He had at last recognized that his work needed to be submitted in typescript. But he had rushed at the serial bullheaded, putting in everything he thought of.

"The art of omission is the hardest of all to learn, and I am weak at it yet," he wrote to Mabel Applegarth. "I am too long-winded, and it is hard training to cut down. As yet, this prevents me from writing perfect little gems, examples of which your brother sometimes sends me."

He set to work, sharpening and cutting his style, giving each sentence the punch of a body blow. But the more he did so, the less happy Mabel became. She preferred writers who could use words like a caress. And apparently editors agreed with her. His stories and articles came back with monotonous regularity. Mabel comforted him by saying that there should soon be a job for him in the post office.

Jack was hurt by her lack of understanding and lack of faith. It changed, but did not lessen, his love for her. He could not any longer look up to her as a sort of goddess on a pedestal. He saw her for what she was, a pretty, middle-class girl with a conventional outlook and rather commonplace mind. He loved her just as much, but pity took the place of respect. If only she would wait, he believed that he would win her over by his success.

He continued to write, pawning first the silver watch that Captain Shepard had given him for the Klondike, then the bicycle that was a present from Eliza, then the raincoat that was his only legacy from John London, and, finally, his only decent suit. He evolved an elaborate method with this pawning. If it was fine, he would pawn his best suit, redeem his bicycle, and take Mabel for a ride. But if he wanted to see Mabel at home, he pawned the bicycle and redeemed the suit.

He experienced all the agonies of poverty. At home there

was never enough to eat. At the Applegarths' there was plenty, but he was too proud to tuck in, because that would have shown how poor he was.

Eliza, then as always, helped not only with her faith in his success but also with any money she could spare; and his mother, perhaps because writing was almost as big a gamble as the lotteries in which she was so fond of buying tickets, gave him her moral support. Jack had read in a newspaper that the payment for 1,000 words was $10.00. As he accumulated his thousands of unpublished words, they dreamed of the money which would roll in when he was accepted.

But the ever-pressing reality was the money pouring out for hire of typewriter and buying stationery and postage stamps. The bill with the grocer mounted to $4.00 and was stopped. The butcher clamped down at $5.00. Jack wrote more and more and ate less and less. He lost weight, felt weak, and became more and more depressed. He thought of killing himself. What stopped him according to one version was the fact that one of his friends came to say good-by before committing suicide and in persuading him not to be such a fool Jack convinced himself at the same time. Another version is that he remembered wading in the sea with a girl and the sight of her feet as she dried them on the sand. As long as there was a girl's foot on earth, he didn't want to leave it. Both stories were obvious simplifications—the truth put in a telling, simple way.

At last there came an acceptance from the *Overland Monthly,* a magazine that had been started twenty years before by the Californian writer Bret Harte. Published in San Francisco, *Overland Monthly* had a good reputation and little money. For Jack's first story, *To the Man on Trail,* the editor of the *Overland Monthly* offered $5.00. It was between 3,000 and 4,000 words in length, and should have brought him over $30.00, if what he had read in the newspaper about magazine payments had been true.

Jack realized that at this stage in his career it was even more important to get his stories printed than it was to be paid for them. Publication was promised for January 1899, and Jack hoped for an immediate payment, since the sum was so small.

But no payment came. Christmas 1898 was perhaps the unhappiest of his life. He couldn't pay the rent on his typewriter, which had to be sent back at the end of the year. He was filled with despair, self-pity, and sorrow at the death of Fred Jacobs, an old college friend, who had died in Manila, during the American seizure of the Philippine Islands. He celebrated Christmas by writing a letter to Mabel in which he unloaded on her some of his own unhappiness.

But the New Year, 1899, opened more brightly. His story appeared in the *Overland Monthly*. Another had been accepted for February. *The Black Cat* magazine wrote to him about a story he had sent them. "They want references, as I am unknown. Then they wish to know if I wrote it myself, if the idea is mine, if it has ever been in print in part or in whole, if it has ever been submitted elsewhere, and if others have or will have a copy of it." It was a science-fiction story which he had written three years before. He thought it was terrible. But his only question was, "Wonder what they'll pay?"

Unlike the *Overland Monthly, The Black Cat* paid quickly —$40.00 for 2,000 words—but held the story for months before publishing it. From the *Overland Monthly* Jack received no payment until he borrowed the money from Eliza to go to San Francisco and call at the office. There he extorted part of the payment due with threats of violence.

Jack did not press his claims as fiercely as he intended,

because he saw immediately that the famous *Overland Monthly* was almost as broke as he was. The editor, Mr. Bridge, was out of town, but he met the assistant editor, Edward Payne, a man of considerable taste and intelligence, and the business manager, Roscoe Eames, a bit of a bumbler, who expressed great admiration for Jack's work.

Like March, he went in like a lion and came out like a lamb, charmed at having met two men so sympathetic with his work. Nothing could be done until the editor came back, they said, apart from printing a third story in their next issue.

At the end of February he met Bridge, who said that he was quite impressed with Jack's second story, but wasn't sure whether Jack could keep up his promise. But he offered to continue printing Jack's stories, giving them a prominent position and drawing the attention of newspapers and reviews to them in order to build up his reputation.

Jack was deeply grateful. He did not realize that Bridge hoped to save his magazine from bankruptcy by printing the forceful stories of this young writer. The average magazine story was nice, homely, trivial stuff remote from real life. Jack London, in comparison, was lusty, powerful, and bursting over with life lived at first hand. The *Overland Monthly* made him known to editors throughout the United States. Here was a young man with something to say and a new way of saying it. Slowly, one after another the editors of magazines with large circulations grew interested in his work and began to buy the stories which he had been trying to sell for years.

One of the first friends whom he made through his writing was Cloudesley Johns, a Californian postmaster, who regarded writing as a vocation he had to pursue, no matter how little he earned from it.

Johns wrote to Jack after he had read his first two stories

in the *Overland Monthly*. He recognized at once that here was a potentially great writer. In the letters that followed the two men explored each other, discovering a great deal in common: the love of literature, the belief in socialism, even such hobbies as chess.

But there was a difference in their attitudes to writing. Jack London had far more talent than Cloudesley Johns, but he had less respect for his art. "If cash comes with fame, come fame," wrote Jack, "if cash comes without fame, come cash." Cloudesley Johns would have said exactly the opposite.

It is always a very difficult thing for a writer to strike a true balance between literature and money. Perhaps the best balance was struck by the writer Evelyn Waugh, who said, "I have never written anything for money; but for what I have written, I always try to get as much money as possible." It is an ideal which few writers can afford to live up to; and Jack London never tried. As a man who from birth had been poor, he wanted money for what it could buy. He sold his talent for putting words together in order to get it; just as he had sold his labor in the cannery, the jute mill, and elsewhere. "I am selling my brains, not my brawn," he said again and again.

And yet this was only partly true. He was an artist, even though he refused to recognize it. However much he pretended that he was "in the writing business" and that the minimum of a thousand words a day which he set himself was as distasteful to him as his work in the laundry, it gave him a secret delight.

His first mistake had been in his attitude toward money, in relation to living. He had to be either a miser or a spendthrift. His second mistake was also in his attitude toward money, this time in relation to writing. Most writers do some sort of "hack" work to pay the rent and family bills, but their "real work" is done for its own sake without regard for the money it makes. Jack London pretended to himself that he wrote only for money, and in the end it became true.

His early letters to Cloudesley Johns, however, were about all sorts of other things: the importance of bravery in a man, the merits of writers such as Robert Louis Stevenson and Rudyard Kipling, criticism of one another's stories, what rates different magazines paid and how long they took to pay, the future of the Anglo-Saxon race.

Jack London had his own ideas about socialism and the Anglo-Saxon race, which Cloudesley Johns did not agree with. Jack had taken over from his mother without any criticism at all her belief that Anglo-Saxons, the English-speaking peoples, were superior to all the other races on earth. From the evolutionists he had taken over the idea of the survival of the fittest. The Anglo-Saxon race, he believed, was the strongest, the most efficient, the fittest to survive. Socialism, he believed, was the best form of government. So socialism would enable the Anglo-Saxon race to conquer the earth and either wipe out what Kipling called "the lesser breeds without the law" or reduce them to slavery.

Cloudesley Johns rightly considered that this was the absolute opposite of the socialist belief in the equality of man. Jack answered, "I do not believe in the universal brotherhood of man . . . I believe my race is the salt of the earth."

These were the confusions of a muddle-headed young man who forgot the fact that he owed most to a black woman, Mammy Jenny, who had suckled him and treated him as her son, and who ignored the fact that he had shown far more sympathy with the Indians in Alaska than any of his fellow white men. It would not be worth while noticing these opinions, if Jack London had ever grown out of them. But they stayed with him for life—apart from a few small changes of emphasis. They were his carefully worked out philosophy; they satisfied his sense of logic. But they ran completely contrary to the dictates of his heart. A great deal of trouble in his life and his work sprang from the fact that he tried to clothe his spirit in a reach-me-down philosophy which did not fit.

But at least in Cloudesley Johns he had found one literary friend. He had plenty of friends of the other sort. While he was trying to work, pals would drift in and waste his time, seamen he had sailed with, hoboes he'd known on the road, college friends, laundry friends, cannery friends—most of them usually coming sooner or later to the point of asking him for money, help, or advice. If he had really believed in the survival of the fittest, he would have told them to solve their own problems (because if they didn't, they were not fit to survive). But he spent hours and days and weeks fighting for others the battles which they were too weak to fight for themselves. His head rejected Christian duty to his neighbor; his heart practiced it.

Cloudesley Johns wrote to Jack in February 1899. In December of that year he met another important person in his life, Anna Strunsky. She was only seventeen, a precocious and very intelligent young Russian Jewess who was a student at Stanford University.

Anna cut across all his ideas about the superiority of the Anglo-Saxon race. She and her family had escaped from the persecution of the Jews by the Russians under the Czar. They believed passionately in the universal brotherhood of man, whatever the color of his skin or whatever his religion. They were universal Socialists, not Anglo-Saxon Socialists. They hated persecution, tyranny, and the superiority of any race or class over another.

Anna met Jack at a Socialist meeting and they were instantly very attracted to each other. "I had a feeling of wonderful happiness," she wrote many years later about their first meeting. "To me it was as if I were meeting in their youth Lassalle, Karl Marx, or Byron, so instantly did I feel that I was in the presence of an historical character. Why? I cannot say, except because it was the truth and he did belong to the undying few."

Jack thought himself engaged to Mabel Applegarth, supposing that he could ever convince her that he was steady and reliable. But he was immediately fired by young Anna. She had the physical passion of Mamie, the culture of Mabel, and something of her own, an independence of thought and talent, which stimulated him—and at the same time made him fight shy. Anna was not feminine. She would not give way. Marriage with her would be a long battle of wills. And Jack liked women who would give way. He told himself that women were inferior to men biologically, just as the lesser breeds without the law (which included the French, Dutch, Belgians, Italians, Germans, Russians, and Scandinavians, as well as Africans, Asians, and Latin-American Indians) were inferior to the Anglo-Saxons.

Anna wanted to be a writer and Jack, who was just beginning to find out about magazines, what they wanted and what they paid, offered to help her. There began a correspondence in which Jack was never entirely at ease. Anna's mind was quick. She reacted faster than any other woman he had ever met. She demanded of him, the great man she thought him to be, a nobility, a self-sacrifice, which he would not give. She thought that his idea of writing for money was a betrayal of socialism.

Anna was right. It was. But then Jack London was not really a Socialist any more than he was a writer for money, though he claimed to be both of these things. He was what he refused ever to acknowledge, an artist unconsciously following his blind destiny.

His tragedy was that he never faced the fact that he was

an artist. He did not even recognize that to be an artist was one of the most sacred vocations there is. He just wanted to make a very great deal of money so that he could have everything he wanted on earth, including Mabel Applegarth.

But as his career opened up, with more and more magazines accepting stories, articles, and even short verses, Mabel grew more distant. Her father died and her mother was forced to move out of Oakland into the country. They had far less money than they expected. Edward Applegarth had left home and Mrs. Applegarth was frightened that she would be left alone in the world without the money to support herself in the position to which she felt she was entitled.

She raised no objection to Mabel marrying Jack, provided that he came to live under her roof. Jack refused because he had his own mother and Johnny Miller to provide for. In that case, said Mrs. Applegarth, she could come to live with Jack. It did not matter so long as Mabel realized that her first duty was to her mother. Jack refused once again. If Mabel married him, she must be his wife first.

Mabel was incapable of choosing between her mother and Jack. She was so sorry for her mother that she could not leave her; yet Jack was the only man she had loved or who had loved her. Why couldn't they all live together?

Jack was adamant. If he was really to win Mabel, she had to come to him. Later, perhaps, they might take her mother in on their terms, but there must be a period alone together.

By mid-February 1900 they had reached deadlock. The Applegarths were forty miles away in San José. Jack was so broke that he had had to pawn his bicycle and John London's mackintosh once more. It would have been inevitable that he should have seen less of Mabel, even if he had not met Anna Strunsky a couple of months before.

His life was branching out in all sorts of ways. His first

collection of Klondike stories, *Son of the Wolf*, was being published in book form. The *Overland Monthly* wanted to claim full credit for having discovered this young writer of genius, and Ninetta Eames, wife of the business manager, Roscoe Eames, was given the task of writing a study of the young man. She invited Jack to luncheon and brought along Charmian Kittredge, her twenty-eight-year-old niece, perhaps with the hope at the back of her mind that the two might strike it off between them. She suggested that Charmian should review *Son of the Wolf* for the *Overland Monthly* and Jack accepted the idea enthusiastically. In a letter to Cloudesley Johns he described her as "a charming girl who writes book reviews, and who possesses a pretty little library wherein I have found all these late books which the public libraries are afraid to have circulated."

Another girl he met was Bessie Maddern, who had been engaged to marry Fred Jacobs, Jack's friend who died in Manila. It was Mabel who asked Jack to see Bessie and console her. But he continued the friendship, because he found in Bessie a nice, quiet, practical common sense which he admired. She was the very opposite of his mother: no hysteria, no fits of rage, no dabbling with spirits. Bessie taught advanced mathematics to would-be undergraduates. She had a well-trained logical mind. Her feet were planted solidly on the earth. She agreed to give Jack free lessons in mathematics in return for free lessons in English literature.

Jack had been deeply attached to Fred Jacobs and Bessie was still in love with Fred. They did not discuss their feelings for each other, but they liked to talk about Fred and their feelings for him. Jack did not feel Bessie was a very exciting or imaginative girl; but she was solid and reliable.

So there in the spring of 1900 were the four women in his life. There was the Lily Maid, the feminine, delicate Mabel

Applegarth, afraid to break from her mother's apron strings. There was Anna Strunsky, challenging, high-spirited with a culture deeper grounded than Jack's, and a fiery personality which he had no hope of mastering. There was charming Charmian, who had all the "advanced" books and a love of dancing and riding horseback and swimming and sailing yachts, a romantically-minded no-longer-very-young young lady. And finally there was Bessie, who was earning her own living by teaching, who knew how to type, was a good plain cook, did not expect anything too luxurious, and was obviously made to be a good mother.

On April 4, 1900, Mrs. Ninetta Eames received a letter which included the following:

> You know I do things quickly. Sunday morning last I had not the slightest intention of doing what I am going to do. I came down and looked over the house I am going to move into—that fathered the thought. I made up my mind. Sunday evening I opened transactions for a wife; by Monday evening had the affair well under way; and next Saturday morning I shall marry—a Bessie Maddern. Also, on said Saturday, as soon as the thing is over with, we jump out on our wheels for a three days' trip, and then back to work.

"Heavens and earth!" exclaimed Mrs. Eames, who had fondly dreamed that Jack would marry Charmian. "The boy must be crazy!"

But Jack London had "read the books." He believed that all the talk about "love" in marriage was nonsense. He did not love Bessie; she did not love him. But in every other way they were made for each other. He sent a letter to Cloudesley Johns by the same post, which ended:

You must be amused before you die. Here goes. You will observe that I have moved. Good! Next Saturday I shall be married. Better. Eh? Will send announcement of the funeral later.

JACK LONDON

Cloudesley Johns was not amused. He wrote back:

May I defer my congratulations of you and Mrs. Jack for ten years? Then I shall hope to tender them—Thursday, April 7, 1910. Don't forget: try to expect them . . . heartily wish you both permanent satisfaction.

CLOUDESLEY JOHNS

10. THE CALL OF THE WILD

JACK AND Bessie had three days' honeymoon and then they returned, he to his writing and she to her teaching. They were to show the world that in the twentieth century civilized men and women did not have to bother about such petty things as love, hatred, or jealousy.

Unfortunately Flora London did not regard herself as a twentieth-century woman. She had encouraged Jack through his years of struggle and now that at last he was beginning to enjoy a measure of success, she was looking forward to her share of it in the comfort of the new house. She was furious that Bessie should move in as Jack's wife and try to take over the management of her home.

Sharing the same kitchen, Flora and Bessie made life hell for each other, and for Jack, who went around to Eliza when things grew intolerable and begged her to keep the peace. The idea of working hard with a wife to whom he was not passionately attached did not seem so good when she and his mother kept interrupting him to arbitrate on their quarrels.

He was earning far more money. He had formed an arrangement with *McClure's Magazine* that they should have first refusal of all his stories. In return for this they paid him $125 a month. Any stories the editor could not use he tried to place with other magazines. When Jack said that he wanted to try a novel, the editor guaranteed him five months' salary on condition that he might see the novel first.

Jack should have been free from money worries. But, like his mother, he always increased his spending the moment he could lay his hands on extra money. As he tried to write this novel, *A Daughter of the Snows,* which combined his experience of the Klondike gold rush with his dream of the twentieth-century woman, he became more and more pressed for money, and had to put the novel aside to do other work to pay his bills.

The squabbles became so violent between his wife and his mother that he took a house nearby for his mother and Johnny Miller and paid her an allowance on which to live. But that did not improve matters. Flora used her allowance for buying lottery tickets and did not pay her bills. When tradesmen pressed for payment, she said her son had turned her out of house and home and gave her no money, and then went around and had a row with Bessie.

Once a week Jack threw his home open to his friends. First among them was George Sterling, a poet with a far greater knowledge of literature than Jack had and whom Jack admired as a man of true genius. Many of them were would-be writers, such as Jim Whitaker, a preacher with seven children, who had given up the church to write novels and to whom Jack devoted a day a week, helping him with his work. There were painters and politicians. Anna Strunsky came from San Francisco with other socialist friends. Mrs. Ninetta Eames would call on her "boy" (as she called Jack rather embarrassingly) and give the latest news of Charmian, who had gone to Europe for a few months.

These Wednesday-night parties were Jack's attempt to ration his friends. He loved company and had a genius for friendship; the only way he could keep time free for his work was by these weekly "At homes."

Bessie did not enjoy them. These hordes of people were all Jack's friends. He was the center of their attention and no one took any notice of her, except when she was providing food. Jack tried to "bring her out," but she didn't want to be brought out. He wanted her to wear smarter clothes; but the clothes she wore and the way she dressed her hair were what Fred Jacobs had liked and so were good enough for her.

They moved from one house to another, each a little grander than the last. The proof of Jack's success was the size of his debts. In the old days his credit with the grocer ran out at $4.00. But soon his debts were up to $3,000. Bessie, used to paying her way, worried at first. But Jack was so confident and impatient of criticism that she ceased to complain. If he said he would find the money, then let him find it. It was no good her trying to save money when he would only squander it in some other way. He wasn't happy unless his credit was pledged to the limit.

Very soon Bessie had another concern which was more important. She was going to have a baby. Jack took it for granted that it would be a son, to whom he could give all the joys of boyhood which he himself had missed. But when a girl was born, he was overcome by the joy of fatherhood. "I did so ardently long to be a father that it seemed impossible that such a happiness should be mine," he wrote to Cloudesley Johns in February 1901. "But it is. And a damn, fine, healthy youngster. Weighed nine and a half pounds at birth, which they say is good for a girl. Intend to call her 'Joan.' Tell me how you like it, what associations it calls up."

The birth of Joan took Bessie still further away from Jack London. Bessie gave more of her love to the baby than to the restless, dominating, boisterous man who was her husband at a moment when his urge to break away was mounting. The pendulum of Jack's life had always swung between responsibility and irresponsibility: from the cannery to the oyster pirates and the *Sophie Sutherland;* from the jute mills and the powerhouse to Kelly's army and the road; from the school laundry to the gold rush. Marriage did not change the pattern of his life. It was three years since he had cut loose; three years of literary drudgery and mounting responsibility. He began to long for an excuse to get away.

The chance came in July 1902. A telegram came from the American Press Association asking Jack to go to South Africa to write a series of articles on the Boer War. Jack cabled his acceptance, packed his bags, and left for New York City next morning.

But the Boer War was dragging to its close. By the time he reached New York the Boer generals were on their way to England to discuss peace terms. Having got so far, Jack was not going to turn back. He proposed to the American Press Association that he should go to London and attempt to interview the Boer generals there. Then he went around to George Brett, of the Macmillan Publishing Company (who had become his publisher in place of McClure's), and suggested that while he was in London, he should go down and live in the slums of the East End and write a book about how the poor lived in the capital of the richest empire in the world. King Edward the Seventh was about to be crowned; and London saw the journalistic possibilities of reporting it not as it appeared in the splendor of Westminster Abbey, but in the squalor of the slums three miles away.

Jack London left his comfortable lodgings and his respectable clothes. He bought a secondhand rig from a pawnshop and went down to live in the East End as an American sailor who had jumped his ship and was waiting for another. He was accepted at his face value, not as a famous American writer; and it is probably true to say that the three months that he spent living in the East End, exploring the grim and poverty-stricken lives of the people there, were in some ways the happiest in his whole writing career. Nobody fawned on him. Nobody tried to borrow money from him. If somebody liked him, it was for his own sake and not because of what could be got out of him.

He felt at home. He had known what it was to be very poor; and he also knew that only among the very poor is

there true charity. *The People of the Abyss,* the book that he wrote denouncing the conditions in the East End of London, was considered in his own time merely as a social document or a piece of political propaganda. But it was more than that. Today what makes it interesting is Jack London's immediate sympathy with the people he met, his appreciation of the children, playing their games in the mean streets, his joy in the triumph of the human spirit.

Much of what Jack London wrote appealed through its violence. But *The People of the Abyss,* laid in a violent setting, appeals because of the tenderness which he saw beneath the surface.

After he had finished his research in the East End he gave himself the short vacation in Europe of which he had dreamed for years. He went to Paris, Berlin, Rome, Naples, and Pompeii. He climbed Mount Vesuvius. Then, hearing that Bessie had given birth to another daughter, he hurried back to be with her. He took with him to New York the completed manuscript of *The People of the Abyss,* together with the photographs which he had taken to prove that what he had said about the slums of the East End was true.

Though he had said, and continued to say, that he wrote only for money, *The People of the Abyss* showed that he did not know what he was doing in following his blind destiny. In the United States it was bound to sell little, because few Americans cared about London. In Britain it was bound to sell even less, because people would resent an American exposing British slums. There was no chance of his making money by selling the serial rights to a rich magazine. But he had written it all the same, out of the righteous indignation in his heart. And it won a place in the hearts of the poor and those who felt for the poor all over the world.

Jack didn't stay long in New York. He wanted to get

back to see his second daughter, called Bess after her mother. He gave the manuscript of *The People of the Abyss* to George Brett, who looked it through and accepted it immediately. He agreed to pay Jack $150 a month against royalties for two years on condition Jack sent him all his books of whatever kind.

And his books were becoming of many different kinds. He had been afraid of becoming typed as a writer of stories about the Klondike. But in the same month that *Children of the Frost* appeared, two other books of his had come out, *A Daughter of the Snows* (as much about modern woman as about Alaska) and *The Cruise of the Dazzler*, a boys' book based on his oyster-pirate days. *The Kempton-Wace Letters* and *The People of the Abyss* showed that he was no mere writer of gold-rush stories.

When Jack got back to the lovely bungalow at Piedmont looking out over the great spread of San Francisco Bay, he discovered that he hadn't appeased his restlessness. Perhaps if Bess had been born a boy, Jack might have felt more settled, dreaming his own dreams into a son. As it was, he found Bessie absorbed in her two babies, content to make her own life with them and leave to her husband his friends, his fight against debt, his public life.

He had discussed a novel based on his voyage in the *Sophie Sutherland* with George Brett, but he sat down to write a short story about a dog, a companion piece to a previous dog story called *Bâtard*. The germ of the idea may have come from a dog he had known during the winter he spent in the Klondike. It belonged to a French Canadian called Louis Savard and its name was "Nig." Half wolfhound, half Newfoundland, "Nig" had hauled Savard's sledge some thirty or forty miles upriver from the Upper Island. Seeing that his master was making ready to return, Nig ran off and came back to camp, leaving Savard to haul the sledge himself. Savard was so furious that he threatened to shoot the dog, but Jack begged him to spare his life.

But once Jack started to work on his story it began to grow. He wrote the 4,000 words (which he had intended to be its total length) and he found that he had only just started on the story. He decided, with that wonder and excitement and fear an author feels when he is possessed by a theme, to let the story take the length it needed. Usually he planned every incident ahead; but in this case he was following the dog into unknown country. The writing of the story was like a voyage of discovery.

At the end of a month he had finished it. It was 32,000 words in length, too long for a short story, too short for a novel. The title he gave it was *The Call of the Wild.*

He corrected the typescript and sent it to Macmillan's, asking George Brett what he thought of it.

It was the first that Brett had heard of it. In New York they had discussed the novel, which became *The Sea Wolf.* There was nothing in their contract about a 32,000-word dog story. It was an unsellable length. But Brett read it and read it again. It was like nothing that he had ever read before, by Jack London or by anybody else. It was unique. As a story it was good, very good. But as a book? George Brett thought long and hard. As a publisher, he could see the critics dismissing it. "Mr. London, having regaled us with the adventures of two young boys in *The Cruise of the Dazzler,* now beguiles us with the story of a dog. He has at last found his level." It could be a howling failure.

And yet it was a challenge to a publisher. To bulk the book it needed illustrations. It must be an adventure in publishing, beautifully and excitingly produced; a tremendous amount of money spent in advertising. And now, as a publisher, George Brett could see an entirely different picture: *The Call of the Wild* a best seller to beat all best sellers—moderately priced so that everybody could afford to be fashionable in possessing it. Even its shortness, then, would be an advantage, because everybody could read it in an hour; and people talk so much more enthusiastically about books they have read than those they pretend to have read.

It was a big risk. He would have to gamble a lot of money if he was to succeed. And in that case, he wanted to make sure that he would get an even greater sum of money in return. He looked at Jack London's contract. For *The Sea Wolf* he was to receive $1,000 as an advance on royalties. *The Sea Wolf* would be anything from 80,000 words upward. George Brett offered Jack London $2,000 for all rights to the book, in addition to the $750 which the *Saturday Evening Post* paid him for magazine rights.

Brett was fair. He explained what he was doing. He might make a great deal of money from the book and he might lose a great deal. Jack was assured of the biggest sum of money he had ever had from a book and that from that time on his name would be known to a far wider reading public.

Broke as usual, Jack London agreed to Brett's terms. But even when the profits of *The Call of the Wild* reached more than a quarter of a million dollars Jack never felt that he had been swindled, or had lost by the deal. Brett had taken a gamble and won. Jack profited from Brett's success with the sales of all his other books.

Apart from the publicity, why has *The Call of the Wild* had this enormous success throughout the world since it was first published in 1903?

The answer is partly that everybody living in civilized or so-called civilized societies feels a secret wish to break away, as Buck broke away, and go back to the wild state away from human cruelty. It is, of course, an illusion that what is wild is better or purer or finer than what is truly human. But there are people either so tame that wild animals appear vital in contrast to them or so beastly that wild animals appear decent.

Yet that is not the only answer.

Jack London prided himself on knowing what he was doing, on being the "master of his fate and captain of his soul." Very often, though not always, when he wrote about human beings, he made them in his own image. They had "opened the books"; they spouted out "modern" ideas as digested by Jack London. Buck couldn't. He was a dog. He could only feel and suffer and fight back. Buck was not the master of his fate and the captain of his soul. He was just a poor, wretched dog, goaded to frenzy by the men around him.

What gave the passion to Jack London's story of Buck's escape into the wild was that in his imagination Jack London himself was Buck.

11. SUCCESS AND FAILURE

GEORGE BRETT's gamble succeeded. *The Call of the Wild* took America by storm. The critics hailed it as a masterpiece. The public, old and young, rich and poor, read it with delight, because its theme appealed to everyone. The name of Jack London stood out as the great hope of the new century's literature. He was head and shoulders above his fellow writers.

Yet Jack London was not a happy man. He had written *The Call of the Wild* out of a deep urge to escape from civilization, or, to be more precise, from the sort of life he led at Piedmont. He realized that he had been crazy to persuade Bessie to marry him. He was honest enough to admit that the blame was his; but that did not make the marriage any better. Bessie devoted herself to the two children. They were the only interest they had in common. But fond though he was of Joan and Bess, they formed a very small part of a busy life, taken up with writing, politics, helping lame dogs over stiles, and his weekly entertainment of the Crowd. Even this busy life began to bore him. It was tame. He was growing soft.

With the check he received from Macmillan for *The Call of the Wild* he bought a sailing sloop called the *Spray*. It had a good-sized cabin in which he could cook and sleep two people. Living aboard the *Spray*, he could recapture the feel of wind and water, which he needed to revive the memories of the *Sophie Sutherland.* It also gave him the excuse for being away from the family and social life of which he had grown tired. It was the one hope of saving his marriage. If only he could loosen the ties sufficiently, they might not chafe and snap.

Yet the time he spent ashore became more and more strained. As Jack's fame grew, the demands on his company became more intense. Journalists from all over the States clamored for interviews. Any celebrity visiting San Francisco was as eager to see Jack London as to see the Golden Gate.

Jack installed two servants and Mammy Jenny to look after the children, but Bessie would have preferred to look after the children herself instead of having to supervise what was almost a private hotel, with flocks of guests appearing at a moment's notice and expecting to be fed. Among those guests were numbers of gay, beautiful, and well-dressed young women, each of whom tried to monopolize Jack. Bessie persisted in wearing her own dowdy clothes and when Jack asked her why she did not read more, she answered that between being awakened by the baby at 6 A.M. and getting to bed at 10 P.M., she had no time to spare from managing the house and looking after his guests.

Jack was still hoping to make a success of the marriage and wrote to Cloudesley Johns: "By the way, I think your long-deferred congratulations upon my marriage are about due. I have been married nearly three years, have a couple of kids, and think it's great." Yet more and more frequently he fell into moods when life seemed pointless. At such times he doubted whether those who called themselves his friends cared for anything except what they received from him in the way of hospitality, help, or money. The men and women crowding his house seemed stupid and he could only tolerate them by nipping off to have a drink.

"What's this chemical ferment called life all about?" he asked Cloudesley Johns. "Small wonder that men down the ages have conjured gods in answer. A little god is a snug little possession and explains it all. But how about you and me, who have no god?

"I have at last discovered what I am. I am a materialistic monist, and *there's damn little satisfaction in it.*" [1]

Even the poet George Sterling, whom he admired and regarded with "honest envy," remained a mystery as a person. "You know that I do not know you—no more than you know me," Jack wrote to Sterling out of his loneliness. "We have never really touched the intimately personal note in all the time of our friendship. I suppose we never shall."

The people who were nearest to him were the *Overland Monthly* group. The magazine itself had folded up. Mr. and Mrs. Eames and Edward Payne had built a house called Wake Robin at Glen Ellen in the Sonoma Valley. It was a gracious place, with beautiful trees and a stream running through the grounds. Beside the stream they cleared a space for a holiday camp, built a communal kitchen, a number of log cabins, and an open-air dining hall with rough wood tables and benches. Edward Payne had at one time in his career been a minister and his plan was to continue his ministry at Glen Ellen, preaching to the summer campers living in tents and the log cabins.

Jack admired the way the two partners, Edward Payne and Ninetta Eames, were organizing the free-and-easy life they wanted. It was just the sort of thing that his mother had tried, and failed, to do. He found in Glen Ellen an approach to the home life which he had never had as a child. Ninetta Eames mothered him, called him her "boy," and, while acknowledging his literary gifts, was never overawed by his fame. Edward Payne, while respecting Jack London as a

[1] My italics. A. C.-M.

writer, thought his "modern" ideas were crude and wrong and was not afriad of standing up to Jack's sledge-hammer arguments.

Finally there was Charmian Kittredge, to whom he had been attracted at their first meeting. Charmian lacked the fire and intellect of Anna Strunsky, but she was his stanch defender, whenever for any reason he was attacked. She admired his work, enjoyed his way of life. Of all the women he'd met, she was the most perfect companion. She was different from the other women in the Crowd. He found himself spending more of his spare time with her, confiding his troubles and ambitions to her, and receiving from her a sympathy that he had sought in vain from Bessie.

During the summer of 1903 Jack's friendship with Charmian deepened. Charmian was convinced that Jack had made a hideous mistake in marrying Bessie and his only chance of happiness lay in his leaving his family and marrying her. Jack was torn between love for his children and loyalty to Bessie on the one hand and his love for Charmian on the other. When at last he made the break with Bessie, he explained nothing of his feelings for Charmian. He dumbly repeated over and over again that they could not go on and next day he removed his things from the bungalow at Piedmont and took a flat for himself, his mother, and Johnny Miller. He slept and worked in the flat when he was ashore, but most of the time he spent aboard the *Spray*, alone or with a friend, such as Cloudesley Johns, pushing ahead with *The Sea Wolf*, short stories, articles, and lectures, and sailing the while.

But although he hid himself, the news of the separation of the Londons spread from San Francisco throughout the United States. Without hard facts the gossip writers were reduced to guesswork. It had been revealed that *The Kempton-Wace Letters* were jointly written by Jack London and

Anna Strunsky; so the gossip writers leaped to the conclusion that it was Anna Strunsky who was responsible for Jack's separation from his wife. Jack denied this, but Charmian would not let him reveal the true reason. She hoped to become the second Mrs. London without taking the blame for ousting the first.

As usual, Jack was short of money. The moment he had finished *The Sea Wolf* he set sail for Korea, to report the war which everybody knew was about to break out between Russia and Japan. He sold his services to Hearst, the highest bidder, but he had other reasons than money for wanting to go. First, he found the strain of keeping his love for Charmian secret almost intolerable. Second, he always wanted to report a war. He felt that if he ever ran dry as a writer of fiction it would be useful to have war reporting as a career to fall back on.

His journey to the war was disappointing. On the voyage out he went down with flu at Honolulu and on the way to Japan damaged his ankle so badly that he could only hobble ashore in great pain. In Tokyo he and his fellow reporters found the Japanese delighted to entertain them but determined to prevent their reaching the war. He set out on his own, was arrested twice: once before he left Japan for taking photographs in a military area and the second time after he reached Korea, in a privately charted junk, for striking a Japanese. He never reached any of the forward areas of fighting, although he got closer than many of his fellow reporters. Finally, having avoided court-martial by the Japanese through the personal intervention of President Theodore Roosevelt, he returned disgusted to San Francisco. The most important thing that he had got out of the trip was a Korean servant, called Manyoungi, the first of a line of Oriental servants whom he employed for the rest of his life.

His reception at San Francisco was even more disappointing. Charmian was not on the quay to meet him. She had gone to stay with an aunt in the Middle West to avoid the least breath of scandal. Instead, he was met by a process server who handed him Bessie's petition for divorce citing Anna Strunsky. The process server told him in the bargain that Bessie had made an attachment on his personal property including his books and any money that he might earn.

Jack hurried to Piedmont and put Bessie right about Anna —but not before Anna's name had been smeared across the United States by the newspapers. When Bessie heard that the woman he had fallen in love with was Charmian, she was appalled, because Charmian had pretended to be her friend even after the separation. "I never care to see her again," she said. But she agreed not to mention Charmian's name in the divorce petition and in return Jack promised to build her a house of her own and make the family a handsome allowance.

Jack went to Glen Ellen and rented a cabin from Mrs. Eames. He had come to regard the place as his home and he hoped that Charmian could be persuaded to stay at Wake Robin. When he wrote, she said that she had no money for the fare. He sent her $80.00. She kept it and said she was frightened of scandal.

Jack felt "hugely disgusted." He had wrecked his marriage for Charmian, but she, afraid that gossip would take the bloom off their romance, would take no risks. He raged and ranted. He fell ill with influenza. He developed a skin disease which made living agony. But Charmian was adamant. She would not come.

The house he had promised Bessie took every penny of his spare cash. But the tide of success was flowing strongly in his favor. *The Call of the Wild* had given his name a magic. His new volume of short stories ran through three printings in five months. Forty thousand copies of *The Sea Wolf* were sold before publication. He was not just a popular best-selling author. He was a literary force. Critics spoke of him in the same breath as Rudyard Kipling and Joseph Conrad. His stories and novels were not merely exciting, they were full of ideas unusual in his fellow novelists. His admirers must have thought that he was rolling in money. But although he had earned $10,000 in the course of the year, he needed $3,000 more to meet his pressing debts by Christmas. Trying to fill his purse was like pouring water into a sieve.

His successes gave him little pleasure. He had lost his family and Charmian would not come to him. He had put her into *The Sea Wolf* as Maud Brewster, and he was bitterly hurt when the critics picked out Maud Brewster as an impossible character.

Charmian came hurrying from Iowa to console him. Her presence in Glen Ellen brought him peace of mind. He started work on a companion piece to *The Call of the Wild*. *White Fang*, as he called it, was the story of a wild dog who comes to live with man. *The Call of the Wild* was Jack London's way of expressing his own desire to break away from Bessie; *White Fang* expressed his desire to settle down with Charmian. It was not so powerful as *The Call of the Wild*, but, like all his writings about animals, had great natural feeling.

Jack spent as much time at Glen Ellen as Charmian thought discreet. He fell in love with the Sonoma Valley. Sonoma was the Indian word for moon and he thought they had called it The Valley of the Moon because its mists shone luminous in moonlight. But the reason why he took the name over was that he wanted some place out of this world of newspapermen and gossip writers, almost on another planet. The Valley of the Moon was a place to start a new life.

One afternoon, when out riding, he came on the perfect

site for a home: 130 acres running from the stream at the bottom of the valley up the side of Sonoma Mountain. It was thickly wooded with huge redwoods, firs, tan-bark, live oaks, madrone, and manzanita. Springs welled from the hill-side and trickled down the narrow canyons; it was the sort of place that would have rejoiced old John London.

Charmian agreed that it was the perfect site for a home, and that very day Jack went over to see the owner, a Mr. Hill, who, Jack learned, had offered the land for sale a few years before for $7,000.

Jack did not possess $7,000; but for 130 acres it was dirt cheap, considering the way land values were going to rise. If he held it for ten years, he would double his money even if he did nothing to improve the land.

But when Jack offered $7,000 for it, Mr. Hill asked him what he wanted to do with the land. The reason why he asked this was that the previous buyer had wanted to develop the water rights. When Jack said he wanted just to farm, Mr. Hill thought it would be swindling to ask more than $5,000. "I reckon you'd better think it over for a few days," he said. He wasn't going to tell London that he was offering too much for the land, but he knew that London had only to ask in Glen Ellen and he would be told what the right price should be.

Jack went back to Wake Robin. He and Charmian and the others spent the evening talking about the possibilities of the place. Jack was furious, as he was sure that Mr. Hill wanted to charge him more than $7,000, because he was known to be a successful writer.

Early next morning he stormed into Mr. Hill's house. "Everyone around here is trying to do me," he shouted. "Seven thousand is the price you agreed to and that's the price I'm going to pay."

There are limits to honesty, and Mr. Hill had reached

them. If Jack London insisted on paying $2,000 more than the Hill Ranch was worth, that was his affair. "O.K., Mr. London," he said. "You shall have it at your price."

Jack rode back to Wake Robin triumphant. Charmian was as unpractical as he was. She thought he had driven a wonderful bargain. While she set to work on the layout of the farm, Jack wrote to Brett to ask him for the $7,000.

By this time Brett had sized up Jack London. He knew that for every dollar he earned he would spend $1.50 or $2.00. That had not mattered so much, when he was spending money in enlarging his experience. But buying land was dangerous—there was so much of it to buy and it cost a great deal to keep. But Jack brushed him aside. "In twenty years' time, Hill Ranch will be worth $120,000."

Brett wasn't interested in what it would be worth in twenty years' time. He was concerned with what Jack would do for money meanwhile. He advanced the money and told Jack that from now on he would have to pay interest on future loans.

Having got the money, Jack was satisfied, except that he was again immediately broke. A lecture agent had fixed up a tour, beginning in Chicago. He would be paid at the end of the tour, but meanwhile he was penniless.

Again he wrote to Brett. "I must pay my way and Manyoungi's to Chicago. Charmian follows in twenty-four hours and there are her expenses. My mother wants me to increase her monthly allowance. So does Bessie. I have just paid hospital expenses of over $100 for Johnny Miller's mother. I have promised $30.00 for printing of appeal of Joe King, a poor devil who has a fifty-year sentence hanging over him and who is being railroaded. There's a bill for over $45.00 for the hay press, and in November I must meet between $700 and $800 in insurance."

Brett must have been tempted to write back and tell Jack

that he should cut his coat according to his cloth instead of demanding cloth for the coats of all his friends. But he knew that there were a dozen publishers ready to provide the money to get Jack London away from him.

Jack London was lecturing on revolution. People were paying big money to listen to exactly the same thoughts that he had been arrested for expressing at the open-air meeting in Oakland. The judge had threatened him with jail if he did it again; but instead of being given jail, he was being paid dollars.

At last, on Saturday, November 18, 1905, more than two years after his separation from Bessie, the divorce petition was granted and next day Jack and Charmian were married. It was a Sunday, and to find a magistrate to marry them was no easy business. The newspapers made the whole thing sound beastly. There was even a suggestion that the marriage was not valid. The scandal that Charmian had been so anxious to avoid blazed up and the smell of it followed them, when the lecture tour and their honeymoon was over, even into the quiet Valley of the Moon.

They decided that it would be a good idea to go away for a time until people had forgotten. They had bought Hill Ranch but it would be some time before it was put into shape. "We're only young once," said Charmian.

"We'll take a boat like Joshua Slocum," Jack said, "and we'll sail around the world. We'll do it slowly. Writing as we go. We'll take seven years over it."

"Yes," said Charmian, "let's."

Jack London felt proud of her as he began to design the boat which was to take them around the world in seven years.

12. THE LAUNCHING OF THE "SNARK"

THE VOYAGE around the world was decided on early in February 1906. Jack London immediately set to work designing his own boat. There were plenty of small boats for sale in San Francisco Bay, and at very reasonable prices. But Jack had his own ideas. He wanted a "ketch," a cross between a yawl and a schooner, with the virtues of both and the drawbacks of neither. She must have an auxiliary engine to steam up the Nile, the Danube, and other rivers. She must have a bathroom, since she was to be their floating home for seven years. She must have a series of water-tight compartments so that she was virtually unsinkable. She must be built of the finest timber. "Spare no money, Roscoe," he said to Roscoe Eames, whom he put in charge of the ketch building at a salary of $60.00 a month. "Put the money into construction. Never mind what it costs to make her stanch and strong; I'll go on writing and earning the money to pay for it."

On February 18 he penned a letter, which he sent to several different magazines. "The keel is laid,"[1] he wrote. "I sail in October. Hawaii is the first port of call; and from there we shall wander through the South Seas, Samoa, Tasmania, New Zealand, Australia, New Guinea, and up through the Philippines to Japan. Then Korea and China, and on down to India, Red Sea, Mediterranean, Black Sea, and Baltic, and on across the Atlantic to New York, and then

[1] It wasn't. A. C.-M.

around the Horn to San Francisco. . . . I shall certainly put in a winter in St. Petersburg, and the chances are that I shall go up the Danube from the Black Sea to Vienna, and there isn't a European country in which I shall not spend one to several months. This leisurely fashion will obtain throughout the whole trip. I shall not be in a rush; in fact, I calculate seven (7) years at least will be taken up by the trip. . . .

"Now to business. I shall be gone a long time on this trip. No magazines can print all I have to write about it. On the other hand, it cannot be imagined that I shall write 50,000 words on the whole seven years, and then quit. As it is, the subject matter of the trip divides itself up so that there will be no clash whatever between any several publications that may be handling my stuff. For instance, there are three big natural, unconflicting divisions: news, industrial and political articles on the various countries for newspapers, fiction, and finally, the trip itself. . . ."

Jack did not want to bind any editor to take his articles if they were below standard. He was confident that he could deliver the goods. But he did want an assurance that he could send series of different articles to different newspapers and magazines. He knew that no magazine could afford to pay enough to cover the cost of the whole trip, including building the boat. But he hoped to get enough different commissions to pay his expenses.

From his point of view it was a reasonable business proposition. But no editor reading his letter could take it as seriously as he meant it. His route, for example, appeared nonsensical on the map. Who in his senses would sail south to New Zealand, then north to Korea, and then south again to India? When he mentioned the Black Sea and the Baltic next to one another, how did he propose to get from one to the other? Did he imagine that they were joined by river and canal? The whole thing was so vague that it did not appear a practical proposition. And anyway no magazine editor could commit himself as far as seven years ahead.

Two magazines betrayed a limited interest, however: *Cosmopolitan* and *Woman's Home Companion*. But although he made it quite clear to each that he was selling them only part of the articles he intended to write, each thought that it was buying all his work and tried to claim the credit of financing the expedition.

The building of the *Snark*, as Jack London christened his ketch after Lewis Carroll's *The Hunting of the Snark*, was cursed with bad luck, bad management, and bad judgment, in about equal quantities. But the initial stroke of bad luck contained the lesson which would have taught Jack London wisdom, if he had only heeded it.

During February and March the material for the *Snark* was ordered and delivered. The keel was to be laid on the morning of April 18, 1906. At a few minutes before 5 A.M., on the morning of April 18, Jack, Charmian, and the others sleeping at Wake Robin were shaken awake. The earth beneath the house began to heave. Then there was a pause. Then the house and the trees outside were shaken like a rat shaken by a dog.

When it was over, and the house had not fallen, Jack and Charmian ran over to the stables, where they found their horses had broken their halters and were skittish and quivering with fear. They rode up to the ranch, partly to see what had happened to San Francisco and partly to find whether the barn which they had had constructed had stood up to the earthquake.

In the dawn light a great column of smoke rose from the city of San Francisco; to the north another column of smoke pillared from the town of Santa Rosa; and immediately below them was a column of dust from the buildings of a state home for the feeble-minded. As for their own barn, which

Jack had told the Italian builder to construct with walls two feet thick of solid rock, regardless of expense, it was a pile of rubble. When they examined the ruins, they discovered that the builder had filled in the center of the walls with the flimsiest of rubble.

Jack was dark with anger. He had paid the man the price he had asked so that he could do a first-class job, but because no one had come down to examine his work, the builder had swindled him. There lay the lesson before his eyes, a pile of ruins. It was no good to tell a man to do a decent job and then go away to earn enough money by writing to pay for it. If he wanted to get value for money, he had to take a personal interest and see he received value for money.

Jack and Charmian rode back, caught a train to Oakland, found that Flora London and Johnny Miller were unhurt, and then caught the last ferry across to San Francisco, where fire was completing the havoc wrought by the earthquake.

They combed the city, looking up their friends to find whether they were safe, and as the fire advanced block by block, wandering dazed and horror-struck through this, the most beautiful city in the United States.

"I won't write a word about this," Jack kept saying. "This is something I can't write about." He had invented terrors of the imagination, had talked with Charmian about what would happen if they were the last inhabitants of a blasted world; and now something had happened which was more poignant than anything they had dreamed of.

At last, in the small hours of the morning, they flopped down on the steps of a fine house on "Nob" Hill and Jack fell asleep. There were many refugees from the poorer quarters sheltering on the steps. The flames were creeping up the street closer and closer.

A man came up the steps, the owner, a Mr. Poring. He saw Jack and Charmian and asked them to come in. He knew the

house was doomed but he wanted to take a last look at it. He took them over the house and showed them his treasures. There was a piano. "Do you play?" Mr. Poring asked.

Charmian was exhausted and it seemed cruel to play when his house would be ashes so soon.

"Do it for him," Jack whispered. "It's the last time he'll ever hear it."

When Jack returned to Glen Ellen there was a telegram from *Collier's Weekly,* asking for an article on the earthquake, offering twenty-five cents a word for 2,500 words. It was the highest figure he had ever been offered, or ever was offered, for an article. And he sat down and wrote the story, handing it sheet by sheet to Charmian for typing.

There was the barn to rebuild and almost all the material assembled for the *Snark* had been ruined.

Jack had given October for his sailing date. He could still have met that date by buying a secondhand craft. But the *Snark* had to be his own creation. The earthquake had created a shortage of labor and all materials. But instead of going down to the shipyard and using all his drive to get the men to work and the materials for them to work on, he retired to his study to write, leaving Roscoe Eames to oversee the boat.

Roscoe Eames was in his sixties. He had played around with yachts as a young man. He had a venerable gray beard, a paunch, and stomach trouble which he treated according to principles of a diet quack named Cyrus R. Teed. "Cellular cosmogony," Mr. Teed called it; and you could take it just as a science, or, if you preferred, as a religion as well. Roscoe took it just as a science, but it did not leave him much time to supervise the building of the *Snark.* He had no control over the men, and as month after month passed Jack took over the building of the boat and told him to go away and learn how to navigate. Edward Payne and Ninetta Eames had persuaded Jack that he would make the perfect captain of the *Snark,* but even Jack realized that to sail across the Pacific Ocean and around the world was more difficult than running a yacht in San Francisco Bay. And that was the extent of Roscoe's seamanship.

If Jack had really supervised the work on the *Snark* after sending Eames off to study navigation he might have produced a decent craft. But he had to write, to lecture, to take Charmian on trips down the coast to George Sterling, to see about the planting of vines and fruit trees for the ranch, and to write violent letters to *Cosmopolitan* and *Woman's Home Companion* about his failure to produce the articles which he had promised on time.

The people who were living off him had increased in number. He had now bought a house for his mother, where she and Johnny Miller and Mammy Jenny lived. Then there were Bessie and the two children in the house he had built for them. He was paying rent to Ninetta Eames and Edward Payne for the rooms he occupied in Wake Robin, where he supported Manyoungi and a cleaning woman. He was paying Roscoe to learn navigation, a foreman and hired men to work the Hill Ranch, to say nothing of all the men at work on the *Snark* who had the idea that they were being paid by *Cosmopolitan Magazine.*

Among his friends the payment of this enormous bill was known as London's Monthly Miracle. It was made. The only thing that made him go on was that Charmian believed that he could do it. She was a very stupid woman, but her faith in him kept him going. She believed blindly that everything he did was right.

The strange thing was that at this moment in his career when he ought to have been writing books which would have been making him a great deal of money he chose to write

Before Adam and *The Iron Heel,* the first about primitive man and the second about a socialist revolution, which he knew would be far less popular than anything he had written before. It was the effect of love. He felt that he couldn't go wrong.

But he went very wrong. By midsummer he had spent $10,000 and the *Snark* was not half finished. By the sailing date of October 1 the bills had mounted to $15,000 and the end seemed no nearer. By the New Year the *Snark* had cost $20,000 and was still on the stocks.

Jack and his ketch were standing jokes. Wisecracks were made about the hastiness of his marriage and the slowness of his departure. With each new announcement of a sailing date friends would lay bets with Jack that he would not be gone by then. Jack took them all and paid up when he lost.

Sincere friends begged him to call the whole thing off before he ruined himself. Old sailors and sea captains examined the craft and went away shaking their heads. If the *Snark* did sail, they prophesied, she would never reach Hawaii. But the whole world knew about the *Snark* by now and Jack felt that he would rather drown than be an international laughingstock.

He decided to sail the *Snark* to Honolulu and finish her there. No sooner had he made the decision than the *Snark* sprang a leak which took days to repair. Then in a storm she was caught and crushed between two barges. Then she got stuck in the mud. Twice a day, for a week, two tugs worked to get her off at high tide. To help them, Jack used his own specially designed windlass. The castings immediately broke and the windlass was ruined. But he still had the 70 horsepower auxiliary engine which had been transported right across the continent from New York. Immediately it was revved up the engine smashed its bedplate, rose up, and sheared all its connections. It lay on its side, a mass of metal useless except as ballast.

By this time $25,000 had been, almost literally, sunk in the *Snark*. Jack complained that contractors, thinking that the *Cosmopolitan* was footing the bill, swindled him by charging treble the proper price or delivering second-rate material for the price of first-rate. But the fault lay with himself for accepting inferior materials and paying bills without inspecting them.

In one of his novels he had remarked that anyone who was really proud was humble and anyone who was really strong was gentle. Although one can admire his spirit in facing setbacks, most were caused by pride that was not humble and gentleness that was not strong. Pride led him to design and build a ketch without the humility of using experts. Gentleness led him to hire Roscoe Eames and continue to employ him after he proved imcompetent. By the time the *Snark* was ready to sail, he had spent $30,000 on a craft inferior to any he could have bought a year before for $5,000. The engine was useless. The power transmission did not work, nor did the motor launch. The lifeboat leaked. Beams he had bought as oak at $7.50 each proved to be pine worth a third of the price. The deck leaked. The sides leaked. The watertight compartments leaked. The specially designed self-bailing cockpit filled with water which would not run away. The gasoline, stored in "leakproof" tanks behind a sealed bulkhead, filtered out, so that it was dangerous to strike a match. The living quarters were awash with bilge on the floor and heady with gasoline fumes below the ceilings. Although the pumps could be kept working to expel the bilge, no air fans had been fitted to expel the gasoline fumes. The tools in the engine room were ruined by bilge water. So were most of the three months' provisions in the galley. The box of oranges had been frozen. The apples went rotten. The carrots tasted of paraffin. The turnips and beetroots were inedible, and the cabbages had to be thrown overboard. Coal had been bagged in potato sacks, which burst in the first storm. The seas washed it through the scruppers.

The special sea anchor designed by Jack to hold the *Snark* without diving was a failure. The first-quality planking from Puget Sound was full of knots and warped. The plumbing of the bathroom backed up after twenty-four hours.

Jack had shown little better judgment in his choice of crew. He had received letters from thousands of people volunteering as crew, many of them offering to pay for the privilege, others forwarding the highest testimonials to their ability. Jack chose Roscoe Eames for his captain. The old man had failed to learn the first thing about navigation. For engineer he took a young footballer from Stanford University who had never been to sea. For cook he engaged a young Middle Westerner, Martin Johnson, who hadn't boiled an egg until he learned of his appointment. They with Jack and Charmian made up the ship's complement. Jack had wanted to take Manyoungi with him also, but the young Korean was even more devoted to life than to his master. He managed to have himself discharged by calling Jack by more and more exalted names such as "Your Majesty" and finally asking him, "Will God have some beer?" This touched Jack on the raw.

The voyage was a nightmare. Captain Eames hid his inability to navigate by announcing that he was constipated and going to bed to eat Cyrus R. Teed's patent health foods. Martin Johnson was too seasick to cook. But this did not matter, as the others were too seasick to eat. When Johnson recovered, he found that the ceiling of the galley was so low that he could not stand upright.

Jack London, the only seaman among them, took his trick at the wheel, two hours on and four hours off. He taught himself how to navigate, steering with one hand and doing logarithms with the other. He taught the others the elements of sailing and at the same time he wrote 1,000 words a day. On the twenty-six-day voyage he wrote *To Build a Fire,* one of the finest short stories in the English language. While he was writing it he and his crew were sailing tropic seas under a blazing sun; yet the subject of *To Build a Fire* was the struggle of a man dying of frostbite in the snows of the Yukon with the temperature at fifty degrees below.

Both Martin Johnson and Charmian London wrote accounts of this voyage. They each paid tribute to Jack London's good humor and his refusal to be rattled by anything except the *Snark's* failure to ride head into the wind. He had considered the specially designed prow, on which he had spent some thought and more money, one of her finest features. Its failure was as total as the bathroom plumbing and the watertight bulkheads and far more dangerous.

Jack knew that their chances of reaching Hawaii were as slender as the old sea captains had prophesied in San Francisco. But he gave no sign of it to the others, except in his delight in discovering on the twenty-seventh day that Hawaii was exactly where he had reckoned it would be.

Jack had visited Hawaii before, as able seaman on the *Sophie Sutherland* and as war correspondent on his way to and from the Russo-Japanese War. His friends welcomed him all the more eagerly because the newspapers had reported that the *Snark* had sunk with all hands in mid Pacific.

Crowds were waiting to cheer them on the quayside of Honolulu. But Jack had the ketch towed to the little island of Hawaii, where a friend had given him the loan of a bungalow. The *Snark* was in no condition to show to the general public.

She had taken a terrible battering and he wanted her repaired and repainted as soon as possible.

The crew was in little better shape. For nearly a month Jack had been living on his nerves without sufficient sleep. His strength was drained, and although he had held up to the end, the first thing that he did on reaching Hilo was to go to bed, where he slept and slept and slept.

13. TROPICAL LIGHT ON A WHITE SKIN

FOR CHARMIAN, Hawaii was a tropic paradise. It was the first time that she had ever seen coral reefs, coconut palms, frangipani blossoms, and dusky beauties wearing necklaces of flowers. And she rejoiced with all her thirty-six-year-old schoolgirl romanticism.

But Jack was met with a pile of letters, which reminded him that however far he sailed there was in California a small army of retainers looking to him for money and that the only way he could pay the wages of his crew, the cost of refitting the *Snark,* and his own personal expenses was by selling his work in the United States.

He had secured a larger sum with the sale of the magazine rights of each successive novel; and although he knew that *The Iron Heel* would be unpopular, as it attacked American capitalism, he had believed, all the same, that he would sell the serial rights for $5,000 or even $6,000. Waiting in Hawaii was a letter from Ninetta Eames, whom he had made his Californian agent, to say that she had tried all the big magazines with *The Iron Heel* and all had rejected it.

"Darn them all," he said, according to Charmian. "They're all afraid of it. They see their subscriptions dropping off if they run it; but they give hell to us poor devils of writers if they catch us writing for the mere sake of money instead of pure literature. What's a fellow to do? We've got to eat, and our families have got to eat."

There was good reason to worry. He had been counting on the money and had already spent it. But the next moment he sent Charmian out shopping, telling her to buy herself anything she wanted. She did so; and perhaps it was the best

thing for her to do. Jack could never have stood a woman who tried to make him businesslike about money.

The Londons spent eight months on the Hawaiian Islands. They were feasted, entertained, and lionized. Charmian kept a lady-like journal of it all, while Jack drank, listened, looked, made notes, and wrote. The most embarrassing thing that happened was when he was introduced to men who had boasted that they had known Jack London well in the Klondike and Jack found that he had never met them in his life. But he always kept up the pretence that he had known them, in order not to make them ridiculous.

What most impressed him was his visit to the leper island of Molokai. Today we know that leprosy is less catching than tuberculosis, and can be cured, if taken early. But in Jack London's time no cure was known and lepers were banished from normal society to isolated leper colonies. Some of his most moving and dramatic stories of the South Seas were written about lepers, who to him were always first and foremost human beings, and only incidentally lepers.

While he was gathering fresh material he supervised the refitting of the *Snark*. Roscoe Eames was sent back to San Francisco. The last straw had been that Eames had not even had the decks cleaned down after reaching port and in the hot sun the seams were gaping.

Questioned in Honolulu why he was leaving, Eames told reporters, "The *Snark* is unseaworthy." When the reporters asked Jack what comment he had to make on this, he tersely answered, "*He* built her."

The engineer left to resume his studies; and when the *Snark* finally left Hawaii, it was with a Captain Warren in command, Martin Johnson promoted to engineer, and an eighteen-year-old Japanese boy, Nakata, as cook.

The eight months spent in refitting the *Snark* proved that her faults were owing not to bad workmanship but bad design. Sailing date after sailing date was postponed, and when they left at last, it was not because they were ready but because Jack could not stand being laughed at any longer. Within twenty-four hours everything had broken down again; and they had to rely upon sail to make the 2,000 miles from the Hawaiian Islands north of the equator to the Marquesas Islands south of the equator.

Jack read in his South Pacific Sailing Directions that it was extremely difficult for a sailing vessel to make the island of Tahiti from Hawaii because of the prevailing trade winds. Tahiti lay to the southeast of Hawaii and although it was easy enough to make southwest, making east on either tack had been found by previous navigators to be almost impossible.

Jack with a combination of luck and good seamanship managed to reach the Marquesas Islands even farther to the east than Tahiti. He was right to consider it as a triumph.

On the voyage to Hawaii they had caught few fish, but from Hawaii to the Marquesas there were so many that they grew tired of just catching fish. They would pick out just *what* fish they were going to catch. And the skill lay in preventing the bait being taken by any other fish. Jack fished for dolphin with rod and line.

"Say, you've seen dolphin," he wrote to Sterling. "Think of catching them on rod and reel! That's what I'm doing. Gee! You ought to see them take the line out (I have 600 yards on the reel, and need it all). The first one fought me about twenty minutes, when I hauled him to gaff—four feet six inches of blazing beauty.

"When they strike, they run away like mad, leaping into the air again and again, prodigiously, and in each mid-leap shaking their heads like young stallions.

"I find it hard to go to sleep after catching one of them. The leaping, blazing beauty of it gets on my brain.

"I never saw dolphins really until this trip. Pale blue, after being struck they turn golden. On deck, of course, afterward, they run the gamut of color. But in the water, after the first wild run, they are pure gold."

In Honolulu Jack had begun a new novel, *Martin Eden.* The name Martin he had taken from Martin Johnson. But the story was the story of his own life when he was studying at high school and university and in love with Mabel Applegarth. He worked on it in Hawaii and on the voyage down to Tahiti. It was the best novel he ever wrote, because it was the only one in which he ever succeeded in portraying an educated woman realistically. Ruth Morse, the heroine, is not interesting as Mabel Applegarth, but at least she is plausible.

Martin Eden was a long novel, 140,000 words in length. Jack had not finished it when they reached Tahiti, where the accumulation of two months' correspondence awaited him.

The shock he had had when reaching Hawaii was nothing compared to what he found in Tahiti. Ninetta Eames had rendered her accounts. She had doubled her own meager salary. She had spent $1,000 enlarging the Hill Ranch building so that the foreman's wife could live with him, another thousand on paying for stores for the *Snark*, a further $1,400 in one month alone for his family, his mother, Johnny Miller, Bessie, the children and Mammy Jenny.

His royalties from Macmillan's had brought him in $5,500. But his balance at the bank was down to $66.00. Nothing was coming in for six months from Macmillan's. The cost of running the *Snark* was $1,000 a month; and because of a rumor that he was dead, one bank had foreclosed on his mother's mortgage and another bank had refused to honor checks he had drawn in Hawaii to the tune of $800.

There was such a mess that the only thing was for Jack to go back to San Francisco to clear it up. The SS *Mariposa* was in Tahiti bound for San Francisco. He decided to go home for a week—and of course Charmian had to come too. On the magic of his name he borrowed the money for their fares. He worked intensively on the novel and by the time they reached San Francisco he had written enough to get money to settle the most urgent debts. He cabled magazines and secured contracts for articles and stories which would keep them going for some time longer. And then at the end of the week he and Charmian boarded the same boat to return to Tahiti.

On the way back he finished *Martin Eden*. When he first proposed to Martin Johnson that he should use him for a hero, he had said, "Of course, I shall have to kill you off in the end."

He killed Martin Eden off by making him crawl through the porthole of his cabin, bound for Tahiti on the SS *Mariposa,* just as he himself was bound. He tried it out himself and then he wrote:

> Turning off the light in his room, so that it might not betray him, he went out of the porthole feet first. His shoulders stuck, and he forced himself back, so as to try it with one arm down by his side. A roll of the steamer aided him, and he was through, hanging by his hands. When his feet touched the sea, he let go. He was in a milk froth of water. The side of the *Mariposa* rushed past him like a dark wall, broken here and there by lighted ports. She was certainly making time. Almost before he knew it he was astern, swimming gently on the foam-crackling surface.

Charmian watched it all. In her childlike way she did not realize how near Jack London was to suicide, nor how blessed a writer is in being able, when he wants to kill himself, to kill his hero.

Jack had been working under terrible strain for years. He had driven himself relentlessly. Captain Warren left the *Snark* at Tahiti and Jack assumed command of his ketch without taking on a mate. They were pursuing the course which he had outlined to the magazines, working west through the Solomon Islands toward New Zealand. A doctor had warned him in Honolulu that in the tropics a man had to take things easier. But Jack had never treated himself just as an ordinary man. He had drawn on his superb strength to do the jobs of half-a-dozen men, and he felt the strain.

On the voyage to the Marquesas he had discovered some bottles of Marsala wine aboard. In the heat it had become very strong and he drank it with a great feeling of power. When he got to the Marquesas, the only pleasant thing he could find to drink was absinthe. It tasted of aniseed. It seemed very weak and he had to drink a lot of it in order to feel any effect. He did not know that it also contained wormwood and when drunk in large quantities it was very dangerous and could produce insanity.

In Tahiti he took on board some cases of whisky and more absinthe. He never made himself drunk, but he needed the stimulus of alcohol to keep going. As well as handling all the ship's affairs he was writing almost as hard during all this time as he had been back in Glen Ellen. And when they made port, it was he who was the center of the entertainment, staying up long nights playing poker and drinking, going out next morning on excursions. He was trying to live thirty-six hours a day. The task that he had set himself of sailing the *Snark* around the world and maintaining all his dependents in California demanded it.

Then a moment came when the dream of sailing around the world became a financial possibility. Ninetta Eames wrote that she had sold the serial rights of *Martin Eden* for $7,000. All his debts were paid, and he had a few thousand dollars in hand to face the future without worry. With this working capital he could have arranged things so that there would not be a crisis each time he opened his mail.

But for months Ninetta had been telling him about the Lamotte Ranch, 110 acres, adjoining his own Hill Ranch. It was for sale for $10,000, a wonderful investment on which he would double, treble, or quadruple his outlay.

Jack's answer to this should have been that he was a writer and he had to sink his capital in writing. But he had always denied his vocation and said that the thousand words he wrote each day was as much drudgery as working in the cannery. He cabled Ninetta to buy the Lamotte Ranch, making a down payment of $3,000 and raising the rest on mortgage. Once again he had his back against the wall.

Tropical diseases attacked them all. They all suffered from bouts of malaria, from perforating ulcers, and the maddening itch of ngari-ngari. Nakata, the cook, nearly went out of his mind with his different afflictions; and it was touch and go whether one of the Polynesian sailors with blackwater fever would survive.

Jack himself stood up better than any of them as far as the Solomon Islands. He stood watch twenty-four hours a day, catching catnaps when he might. He was ship's doctor as well as captain and mate; and every day he ground out his thousand words except when he was too ill with fever, and a couple of times when nasty squalls hit the *Snark*.

But when they reached the Solomon Islands Jack was struck by a disease that he found as mysterious as it was painful. His hands swelled and became so sore that he could not close his fists. The skin began to peel, one layer after another. It grew silvery, like Naaman's leprosy in the Bible. The nails on his fingers and toes grew hard and thick—as thick, Jack said, as they were long, and when they were filed, were as thick again next day.

A sudden panic came over him that he had contracted leprosy. He asked the old-timers if they had seen any condition like his, but they hadn't. Many of them were hard-drinking men. And they did their jobs as diligently as they could. But none of them had ever tried to sail a ketch as master and mate, doctor the crew, and run the business of being the most productive writer in the United States, supporting a dozen people from the South Pacific.

His hands grew so sensitive that it was agony to touch anything. His sense of balance was affected and he was afraid of walking. His body was seized with nervous attacks and his mind was filled with dark thoughts of persecution. He had set himself up as a man superior to others. If he achieved what everybody said was impossible and sailed the *Snark* leisurely around the world, he would have proved that he was no ordinary man. Now his body was stricken with this strange disease, he had the delusion that it was a plot on the part of his enemies to prevent his completing the voyage. But he swore they would not succeed. He would take a steamer to Australia, recover his health, and then return to resume the voyage.

The trouble developed on his hands and feet in mid-September, when they were at Guadalcanal in the Solomon Islands. No steamer was due until November. Meanwhile he joined with a company of "blackbirders." The solemn description of "blackbirding" was "the recruitment of labor to work on plantations." Raids were made on primitive islands, inhabited by naked cannibals. Men were taken by persuasion or by force and sold to plantations on neighboring islands. These "labor recruits" were given three-year contracts at a low wage, so that they were technically not "slaves." But if they tried to escape and were recaptured, their wages were deducted and they were forced to serve another year or two. It was a traffic as morally degrading to the men who practiced it as it was physically degrading to the unfortunate victims. Yet surprisingly Jack and Charmian felt no disgust, indignant though they were at the conditions of the slums of East London and of children working in American factories.

By the time the SS *Nakomba* put in at Guadalcanal Jack London was a sick and frightened man. Twelve days later he was in a Sydney hospital. "I am as helpless as a child," he wrote. "On occasion my hands are twice their natural size, with seven dead and dying skins peeling off at one time." The Sydney specialists confessed that they did not know what was wrong with him or how long it would be liable to last. After five weeks in a hospital and a further five in a hotel he abandoned the idea of continuing the voyage around the world. Martin Johnson was sent to bring the *Snark* from Guadalcanal to Sydney, where at a public auction it was sold to a "blackbirder" for less than one tenth of what it had cost him to build.

The voyage which had begun as an escape to paradise had ended in hell. All Jack's previous adventures had been distinguished by the quality of pity, which found goodness in tramps and jailbirds, pirates and pugs. But in the Solomon Islands he had committed the greatest crime of man against man. He had hunted fellow human beings to make them slaves. As if in retribution he had been stricken by a disease that hit at the foundation of his pride, his physical strength.

The illness was not pure waste. It taught him the frailty of man and inspired him to write one of his greatest short stories, *A Piece of Steak*, based on his own sickness, and the fight between Burns and Jack Johnson, which he reported in Australia. It was the story of an old boxer being beaten by a young man and realizing in the moment of defeat how the old boxer he himself had beaten as a young man must have felt when he burst into tears. It was Jack's first recognition of the tragedy of age and failing power.

From Australia they came slowly home, spending a few weeks in Ecuador on the way. There he saw a bullfight, the cruelty of which filled him with an indignation he had not felt against "blackbirders."

They reached Wake Robin in July 1909, twenty-seven months after they had set out from San Francisco. During that time Jack had written six books, the greater part of a seventh, and a number of stories and articles which were published in later books.

It would have been a remarkable achievement, if he had been sitting at home, enjoying the best of health. It was fantastic for a man who had been at the same time living so hard, working so unremittingly, and laboring under such bad health.

It should have meant that he came back to find things at least financially easier. But the tangle was worse than ever. The only thing that consoled him was that the strange swelling of his hands, the peeling and the thickening of his nails, gradually cured themselves. And on the voyage home he discovered what he thought was the cause of his strange disease. It was merely the effect of tropical light on a white skin. He had had no reason to be frightened of some unknown form of leprosy.

So he went back to his old way of living, unaware that what he had really suffered from was a form of pellagra, a disease made worse by exposure to sunlight, brought on in heavy drinkers by a lack of Vitamin B.

14. HOME TO STAY

AT WAKE ROBIN Jack found that there were changes. Ninetta Eames was divorcing Roscoe and going to marry Edward Payne. There had been violent disagreements between Jack and Ninetta while he was away. But he recognized that they were more his fault than hers. His agent in New York City had been selling his stories in one market while Ninetta had been selling them in another.

To avoid further confusion, he recalled every unaccepted manuscript and wrote around, saying that he had magnificent new material, that he was home to stay, and in future there would be no more misunderstandings.

For three months not a word was printed under Jack London's name for the first time in nine years. During his absence his reputation had fallen—as much as anything because he had been absent. There had been few mentions of his name in the press. What there had been were unfavorable. His second marriage and the voyage of the *Snark* had had a bad press. Editors and critics had decided that he was written out and that the public was tired of him. Jack knew that this wasn't true, and he set to work to make his reputation all over again.

Today *Martin Eden* is considered to be his best novel. But when it was published, his publisher could not find any words of praise to quote in his advertisements.

It fired Jack to have to fight his way up to the top again. He sold *A Piece of Steak* for $750 to the *Saturday Evening Post* and secured a contract for twelve stories to be delivered during the following year. He sold the serial rights of *Burning Daylight* for $8,000 to the New York *Herald.* The *Herald* bought for this the right to sell reprint rights in other American newspapers, and every newspaper that took the serial wrote articles boosting Jack London. His stock began to rise rapidly. He knew that he had not lost his touch.

Then Charmian gave him the news that delighted his heart. She was going to have a child. He felt the loss of Joan and Bess more than he had realized. He immediately launched into plans for the home in which they would spend the rest of their lives.

Just as he couldn't sail around the world in a boat that had been built by anyone else, so he couldn't live in a house that had not been constructed to his own design. He wasn't an architect, but he and Charmian found a site on the Hill Ranch, up toward the crest, looking right out over the hills to the sea in the distance. It was surrounded by redwoods, the clearing of which for the site and the view gave timber for the woodwork; and on the estate there was plenty of rock. It was to be built solid out of the rock and the timber of the estate, so solid it would stand even against earthquake.

He decided to call it the Wolf House. In his letters to George Sterling he signed himself Wolf. It was the word the Indians of Alaska used for the conquering white men. And he had taken it over in *Son of the Wolf* and *The Sea Wolf.* He himself had been a lone wolf, running between the tame and the wild.

He called in architects and explained what he needed. Wolf House was to be tailored to his needs. There were four thousand books, stacks of cardboard boxes with reports, newspaper clippings and pamphlets, thirty high rows of black boxes in which he filed mementoes of his travels and his accumulations of games, jokes, puzzles, and practical jokes. He had to have room to entertain and to work while

Charmian was entertaining, and a music room in which Charmian and their musical friends could play and a dining room in which he could seat fifty people, and kitchens and bedrooms and all the other aids to gracious living.

His own birth had been obscure. He had never found for certain who his father had been. But there was going to be no doubt who was the father of Charmian's child. Wolf House was to rise as the ancestral home of the first of the great London dynasty.

In charge of construction he put an Italian master stonemason called Forni, from the nearby town of Santa Rosa. He told him to build a house that would stand for centuries. To make the joints firm against earthquakes, the rock had to be washed and scrubbed with a wire brush before laying. Extra cement was to be used for the mortar, and one man's job was to keep the walls wet to prevent the cement drying too quickly. Only the very best and most lasting materials were to be used. To get work finished as soon as possible, he told Forni to employ thirty workmen. But even so he knew that he was fighting a losing battle. To build an ancestral home to last centuries takes longer than having a baby.

Before the baby arrived, Jack gave a home to his stepsister Eliza. She was forty-three and her husband was now seventy-one. She had never been very happy with a marriage that had been made merely to get away from drudgery. There were only two people whom she loved, Jack London and her son, Irving Shepard.

The cost of building Wolf House was reckoned at $30,000. It might be thought that this was enough for even Jack to undertake. But as soon as he took Eliza to manage for him, he bought another property, the Kohler vineyards, which joined up the Hill Ranch and the Lamotte Ranch. It covered 800 acres and cost him another $30,000, which he did not possess.

As people grow older they often become more and more like their parents. Jack London had always shared his mother's habits of extravagance and gambling on the future. And the older he grew, the more reckless he became, persuading himself that turning the short stories he spun out of his brain into acres of forest, vineyard, orchard, and plowland was a sound investment. It was realizing John London's dream and Eliza Shepard shared it with him. Charmian looked on and admired, but she had little to do with the farm, the typing of Jack's manuscripts and letters being her job.

In June 1910, while Jack was frantically writing to his publisher for the $10,000 which he needed for a down payment on the vineyard, Charmian went to a hospital in Oakland to have her baby. Once again it was a girl.

But this time the baby lived for only three days.

To both of them it was a terrible grief. They had reached a point in their marriage where both of them felt the need for children; and Charmian, knowing Jack's passionate desire for an heir, felt that she had doubly failed him.

But there was still time. Forni and his laborers continued their work on the house. Jack redoubled his efforts at writing, steadily increasing the rates which he received from magazines, grinding out bad work and good, and being paid handsomely for all of it.

He gradually turned aside from people; apart from a small group of artists, writers, and "sages," who had nothing in common except that they amused Jack and enjoyed taking his hospitality, he took pleasure in few of the people he met. They were always sponging on him or cheating him. The idea of reforming society through socialism no longer interested him very much. The change, he decided, had to start on the land, his land. When he had taken it over, the land had been run down by bad farmers, who took more out of the soil than they put back; snatch-crop farmers who wrecked a farm in a few years and then moved on to wreck another farm.

All his spare time Jack spent in reading books and government reports on farming. On the hill fields he introduced "contour plowing," plowing along the line of the hills in terraces to hold the rain on the land and prevent the topsoil from being washed away. He grew crops to build up the fertility of the soil and introduced the first manure spreader on the West Coast to bring the animal manure to the land before it lost its strength. He blasted rock that he crushed in his own stone crusher and built a dam to make an artificial lake to increase his irrigated land. He built the first silos for storing his and his neighbors' grain. He bought prize shire horses and bulls and boars for breeding. He designed his own piggeries, in which the pigs were self-fed from a central chute and the sties self-flushed "as sweet as a nut."

His farming was, as someone called it, "an act of creation." He was creating a man-made Garden of Eden which he hoped would serve as a model to other American farmers.

But it did not bring an immediate return on the money that he sank in the ranch. He paid his workers more than the usual wage, but he got less than the usual work from them. His men knew that he was a writer by profession. His farming, though far more scientific in principle than that of his neighbors, was all the same a rich man's hobby. They respected a farmer, who was always on the land himself, who sweated his hands as hard as he sweated himself. But they despised an owner who never did a hand's turn himself and who was away from his ranch for months on end. Hard as Eliza worked, it was impossible for her to oversee the running of the farm, the ranch house, and the building of Wolf House.

Jack London's belief in his fellow men sank lower and

lower. "The more I see of men," he said, "the more I turn to the land; yet, in order to manipulate that land, I must deal with those very men who hurt me so with their blind ineffectiveness and lack of foresight." Yet it was his own lack of foresight that made him devote so much of his time to the writing which he said he loathed to pay for the losses on the land he loved.

During 1910 and 1911 Jack acted as if he were "at home for good"; but in 1912 he and Charmian made the voyage which he had dreamed of making all his life, westward from Baltimore around Cape Horn in a four-masted barque, one hundred and forty-eight days at sea.

One of the reasons for his making this voyage was that he had found in the United States that he had come to rely more and more upon alcohol. He had begun to suspect that he might not be able to do without it. But he drank nothing on the voyage and by the time he had worked the whisky out of his system he had decided with relief that he was not an alcoholic. He was able to control himself.

But although he told this to Charmian and even partially convinced himself, he started work on his famous alcoholic memoirs, *John Barleycorn*, in which he told the story of his own drinking life and pleaded that the sale of alcohol should be prohibited in the United States.[1]

When they returned to Glen Ellen, Jack London had conceived a new sea novel based on the voyage around the Horn, *The Mutiny of the "Elsinore."* Charmian was expecting another baby but to their grief she lost it within a month of returning home, through bad doctoring.

Life is an art. Jack had tried to swagger through it, playing

[1] *John Barleycorn* played a very big part in introducing prohibition into the United States after World War I. Instead of preventing drinking the effect was to increase the amount of drunkenness and to encourage the growth of organized gangsterdom. Although prohibition was repealed in the 1930's, the rackets that began with "bootlegging" still survive in other spheres.

it as a game, a rough game like boxing. And as he had foreseen in *A Piece of Meat,* the time comes in a boxer's life when he is beaten.

All his life he had dreamed of having children. There was a passage in the diary he kept as a tramp of nineteen where he was suddenly overwhelmed by the desire to be a father, to have children whom he could love and cherish and educate.

Although he continued to love Charmian, he began to despair of her giving him children, and he thought more and more of Joan and Bess, the two daughters whom he had given up to Bessie in order to marry Charmian. He had begun to make approaches to them after he returned from the *Snark* voyage. He would go to see Bessie and play with the children. Bessie agreed to this, because, although she was bitter in her heart, she had a sense of what was just to the children's father.

What she resisted was Jack's pressure that the children should come out to the ranch. She was afraid that Jack would take her daughters away from her with the lure of all the lovely things he had there. She went once with them to the ranch on a picnic. They had the cloth laid and all the food laid out when Charmian rode up and her horse kicked earth all over the food. Perhaps it was accidental, but the two wives hated each other and this incident summed up their hatred. Bessie said she would never take the children back to the ranch, although Jack was welcome to visit at Piedmont whenever he wished.

Meanwhile the Wolf House slowly rose in its magnificence. It was the one hope that seemed to flourish. That and the ranch, to which Jack added another 400 acres on mortgage.

He was working well. He wrote *John Barleycorn, The Mutiny of the "Elsinore,"* and *The Valley of the Moon,* the first part of which was a magnificent story of teamster life in Oakland and the second part of which was a very interesting treatise on farming of California, which had nothing to do with the first part.

Jack was still growing as a writer. He was less interested in writing about city life, less certain that the revolution which he had preached when he was younger would solve all the ills of mankind. He was more interested in the land and the revolution needed in methods of farming. His old friends, the Socialists, who had proposed him as Socialist candidate for the presidency of the United States, thought he was "going off" as a writer. But his new friends, the forward-looking farmers and stock breeders, the hundreds of thousands trying to win a living from the soil, saw him as a sort of prophet. It is the inevitable thing with all writers that they should develop, and in developing they should lose old friends and make new ones. And as the old friends lament the loss of a good comrade, the new ones welcome an ally who has at last found the light. Just as agriculturalists said that *The Valley of the Moon* should be a textbook in all farming colleges, so teetotalers pounced on *John Barleycorn*. Preachers based sermons on it. Prohibitionist societies quoted it in pamphlets. Lecturers took it as their illustration of the evils of drink.

Jack's stature as a public figure grew larger during the year 1913. It was the height of his fame. He had never been so successful.

But it was also the most disastrous year in his private life, a long succession of misfortunes.

It began with the illness of a woman he knew. She had been an invalid for some time, and then she took a turn for the worse. He could not pray for her because he did not believe in prayer. But "I did something last night I never did before," he told Charmian. "I concentrated every thought and actually tried to call that girl back. If anyone could, I think it would be myself. . . . Of course there was no answer."

Then Eliza's son was nearly electrocuted and lay in the London house for months precariously ill.

Jack himself had to be rushed to the hospital and operated on for appendicitis.

One of the most valuable draught brood mares, in foal, was found dead in the pasture. Somebody had shot her during the night.

The early rains failed. A false spring brought blossom and fruit on too early and it was killed by frost. Then a plague of grasshoppers came and consumed even the baby eucalyptus trees he had planted.

He became involved in a lawsuit over the control of the film rights of *The Sea Wolf.* He was sold some Mexican land stock that he thought would bring him a fortune and landed him in a loss. Another fraudulent gamble caught him immediately afterward, and between the two of them he lost $10,000, just as his mother had lost far smaller sums in the past.

The Wolf House was still not finished, and on August 18, 1913, with only $300 in the bank and big bills to meet, Jack mortgaged everything he could lay hands on, so that he could have the Wolf House finished by winter. The bank insured the Hill Ranch for half the amount which they had loaned, but there was no insurance on the Wolf House, because it was obvious that a great square block, built of stone and concrete, with massive redwood beams, could never burn down unless it was deliberately set fire to in a dozen places at once.

Yet that was what happened four nights later, on August 22. Forni, the builder, had spent the evening discussing the details of finishing the job and moving the Londons' furniture. At eleven at night he went back past the house on which he had spent three years of his life. He went to sleep in his cabin, but three hours later he was awakened by a farmer hammering on his door, shouting, "Forni, it's burning! The Wolf House is burning!"

Forni leaped from his bed, pulled on his clothes, and ran down to the house, but by the time he reached it flames were everywhere. Every room in that stone palace built to last a thousand years was ablaze. And what was suspicious was that even the cut redwood planks stacked in a clearing beyond the trees which surrounded the house were blazing also.

Jack and Eliza had seen it from the ranch half a mile away. Charmian joined them. Her impulse was to rush to the scene of the fire. But Jack was more cautious. He knew that there wasn't a chance of saving the place if someone had deliberately fired it—just as someone had shot the brood mare. While Charmian gave orders for the teams to be harnessed, Jack instructed his servant, Nakata, to keep an eye out for anyone who might try to set fire to their ranch house while they were away. "What's the use of hurry?" he said. "If that is the Big House burning, nothing can stop it now."

He was right. Nothing could. They went up. All the neighbors came around. Forni and his workmen stood watching their handiwork go up in flames, almost demented.

"Why don't you cry, or get excited, or something?" asked one of the neighbors.

"What's the use?" asked Jack, too sad for tears. "It won't rebuild the house."

15. THE RUINS

THE FIRE was on a Friday night. For two days the Londons and Eliza, who had supervised the building throughout, felt shattered. Jack reckoned that he was $100,000 in debt. He could have declared himself a bankrupt, but he refused to default on his debts. Somehow or other they would be paid; although when he thought of the thousands of words he would have to write, he felt very tired.

By Monday he had realized that there were other people who had suffered almost as deeply as himself. Forni, the master builder, had thought on, worked at, and dreamed of this house for three years. It was his chance of fame, the house that was to stand a thousand years. The Martinelli brothers, two of his best men, had stood watching the flames, the tears streaming down their faces, crossing themselves and muttering, "O Jesus! O Mary, Mother of God!" These men were waiting upon him, as if the end of the world had come, and wondering what would happen next.

The world outside was watching also. The Wolf House had been written about in hundreds of newspapers. It was the symbol of the life work of Jack London, the poor sailor boy who had become the most famous writer in the world.

It had become a symbol, but exactly what sort of symbol was not clear to people. The bums, the convicts, the workers and the workless, the Socialists, the poor, and the oppressed were puzzled that their champion should build himself a house to rival those of the railroad kings, the captains of industry. It seemed to many of them wrong that a man should have become so rich by sticking up for the poor. But to others it appeared a proof of how wrong Jack London's socialist ideas were. How could he say that there were no opportunities for the poor to rise in the capitalist United States, when that was what he himself had done?

Perhaps it was one of these disgruntled people who had set fire to the house. The culprit was never discovered. But meanwhile millions waited to see how the writer would stand up to the blow.

On Monday Jack told Forni that his work would be paid in full and meanwhile he and his workmen were to build a splendid retaining wall of mossy gray stone on the right of the drive to the ruins, which were still smoking. The world had not come to an end. Life was to go on as normal.

But within himself Jack knew that life would never be the same again. He had toiled and sweated to create in stone something that would stand for centuries as beautiful, and then some enemy, whom he did not even know, had destroyed it in a night.

He was filled with bitterness against the world of men and women to whom he had given of his riches, because he thought they were his friends. He remembered once recently when Charmian had asked him for $300, which he hadn't at hand, he appealed to these friends (to whom he had "lent" over the years more than $50,000 on the promise of repayment later). In response to his appeal he succeeded in borrowing $50.00. He had cast himself for the role of prince; and no one would accept him as pauper. He had lost his friends because he had made himself too big, too rich a man for friendship. In friendship there is give and take. But he had proudly given too much and accepted from his friends too little. He had turned them into spongers.

What hurt him most of all was that there was not a single word of sympathy from his daughter Joan. She was thirteen and old enough to understand what the burning of the Wolf House meant. He wrote to her, reminding her that he was her father, had fed, clothed, housed, and loved her from the moment she was born. "What do you feel for me?" he asked. "Am I a fool who gives much and receives nothing? I send you letters and telegrams, and I receive no word from you. Am I beneath your contempt in every way, save as a meal ticket? Do you love me at all? What do I mean to you? I am sick—you are silent. My home is destroyed—you have no word to say. The world does not belong to the ones who remain silent, who by their very silence lie and cheat and make a mock of love and a meal ticket for their father. Don't you think it is about time I heard from you? Or do you want me to cease forever from caring to hear from you?" He forgot that his daughter saw him as a man who had abandoned her mother years before.

Charmian, whom he had found a delightful companion, sailing, riding, and traveling, did not help him in his darkness. Although a woman of forty-three, she had not matured over the years—partly because Jack himself never took her fully into his confidence about his worries; he had never treated her as an adult woman. She still behaved like a young girl, with coy tricks which in a young girl are charming but in a woman in her forties acutely embarrassing.

One evening, as Jack and Eliza were working together trying to see some way out of his immediate money troubles, in flounced Charmian draped in velvet cloth. "Won't this make a gorgeous outfit?" she cried, as she strutted up and down. "I've just bought two bolts of it." After she left the room there was a long silence, broken by Jack. "She's our little child, Liza," he said. "We must always take care of her."

Charmian was the nearest approach to a little child that he ever came to, though he continued trying to win his daughters over. A year after the burning of the Wolf House Joan sent him a play which she had written. "I like it tremendously," he wrote back, "and can hardly believe that I am the father of a girl who is so big that she can write such a play."

For some months he kept up the correspondence and then he went to see Bessie at her house in Piedmont to put a business proposition to her. According to his will he left everything to Charmian. But if Bessie would let the children come up to the ranch and get to know their father again he would make a new will leaving the estate to the two girls. He would build Bessie a home in a protected corner of the ranch. Bessie could always be with the children to make sure that Charmian would not interfere. In fact, he would agree to any conditions she wanted, provided that he could have his daughters back.

Bessie refused. Her children were all she had to live for and she was even more frightened of Jack's love for the children than of Charmian's dislike for them all.

A few days later Jack appealed directly to Joan. "It is a hard proposition to put up to you at your age, and the chances are that in deciding on this proposition I put up to you on Sunday night you will make the mistake of deciding to be a little person in a little world. You will make that mistake because you listened to your mother, who is a little person in a little place in a little part of the world, and who, out of her female sex jealousy against another woman, has sacrificed your future for you. I offer you the big things of the world, the big things that big people live and know and think and act."

This letter of Jack's shows how sick in spirit he had grown to think that the "big things" he offered were greater than love. Joan did not answer this or several other letters that followed; but at last she replied that she was happy at home, that she would stay with her mother always, and she resented what he said about Bessie, whom she loved because she was a good mother, and she hoped he would never force her to write another awful letter like this.

And so Jack London was left, a very lonely and loveless man, in his big world, where he was known to thousands and read with admiration by millions.

There remained to him little that brought satisfaction. Occasionally his work flared with the old fire. He had petitioned for years to get a man named Ed Morrell out of San Quentin Penitentiary, where he had been kept for five years in solitary confinement. At last his efforts were successful and Jack had Morrell out to stay on the ranch, where he pumped him for material about prison life. With this material he produced his last great novel, called in the States *The Star Rover* and in Britain *The Jacket.* It was a denunciaof the prison conditions, about which Jack had felt passionately ever since his own short term for vagrancy. But he lit the gloom of its theme with a series of imaginative flights backward in time, illustrating the theme of man's inhumanity to man throughout history.

There were also, right up to the end, short stories in which he revealed that he had not lost his mastery. But he was running short of ideas and bought a number of plots from a young writer named Sinclair Lewis, who was to make a reputation for himself later on with *Babbitt, Main Street,* and other satires on American small-town business life.

His life fell into a pattern. Three to four months were spent each winter in Hawaii; the rest of the time he was based on the ranch, making business trips to Los Angeles about film rights and to New York City about his books. He was still in his thirties, but he had lived so hard that he looked older. He had put on fat and he no longer delighted in physical exercise. He felt ill and drank whisky to make him feel better, but when the effect wore off he felt worse. He had been able to drink a great deal in the past without showing any sign of drunkenness. But now his friends saw him drunk.

His judgment was affected. He started speculating. He loaned his name to a company for marketing grape juice. Two friends were to put up the money, but he soon found himself in court sued for a large sum of money. He bought half an interest in a gold mine in Arizona that did not exist. He sold stories to film companies for a share of profits that were never made. He bought a story idea he didn't need from his old friend George Sterling, because he knew Sterling was hard up, and then heard that Sterling was criticizing him for "selling out" to the commercial papers.

The only things that seemed pure and true were the ranch and Eliza's devotion to it. The land was a bigger, better thing than the men who grubbed a living from it. He gave his best to improve the ranch, making it ever more fertile. He planned to raise the height of the dam, so that his artificial lake could irrigate still more land.

Then, to his surprise, he found that there was a petition among his neighbors to prevent his doing this on the grounds that he was taking their share of the water. To his grief he discovered most of the neighbors had no feelings themselves about the dam, but had been egged on by Ninetta Eames and Edward Payne, two people whom he felt that he could trust almost as completely as Eliza. It seemed to him the final treachery.

On the last day of the court case he gave evidence for four hours, fighting against the people he had thought were his friends. He was in great pain, his body swollen with uremia. But he carried on, not realizing how ill he was. His plan was to go to New York City for a spell without Charmian, who was feeling ill.

On Monday, November 21, Jack worked during the morning. In the afternoon he asked Charmian to ride up the mountains with him to look at some land that he wanted to buy for its water rights. Charmian excused herself, because she was too weak for a long ride.

He came back later very pleased and excited. He had found the land and the name of its owner. He intended to make an offer for it, when he had sold some work in New York; perhaps the autobiography he planned to write called *Sailor on Horseback.*

That night he did not sleep. Usually he woke at 5.30 A.M. and started to work. But next morning he rose late and he wrote only a few pages in the morning and dictated few letters.

He did not go out all day and slept all the afternoon. He found it hard to rouse himself, but when Eliza came over to talk ranch business he became very excited, talking about the future of the ranch. He wanted to set up a ranch store, a school, and a post office as soon as possible and gave Eliza instructions on how she should do it while he was away.

"There are enough children on the ranch to open a school," he said. "The ranch people can have their homes here, trade here at better prices, be born here, grow up here, and if they die, and so they wish, they can be buried on the Little Hill. . . ."

Eliza was worried not by his plans but by the feverish way he was developing them. After the sluggishness of his awakening it was like a mental fever.

He was late for dinner and he did not want to eat. For a time he talked, becoming angry over a man who had come into the hills hoping to buy land when the slump came and then make money out of reselling it in small plots later on.

Charmian asked him whether he would like her to play

for him. But his mood had turned dark. He was tired and went out to the sleeping porch with a pile of books.

Charmian went out for a walk in the starlight. When she came back it was about nine. Jack's light was burning. Tiptoeing across, she saw from his own room that his head had fallen on his chest, the eyeshade down. He made a slight movement as if settling to sleep. She did not go in to kiss him good night for fear of waking him, but went to bed, read for a few moments, and soon fell fast asleep, "the first unbroken eight hours' sleep in weeks."

By seven o'clock next evening, Jack London was dead.

* * * * *

Every writer, or public figure, is two people. He is the private person, as he appears to himself and his family and friends; and he is a public person, usually quite different, as he appears to those who have only known him from afar through his books and his public reputation.

This life of Jack London has been primarily concerned with Jack as a private person, the boy who never had a boyhood because he was always trying to be older than his age, and the man who never grew to full manhood because he was always trying to recapture the boyhood he had never had.

Like all human beings, he made a great many mistakes. His mistakes, because he was a great man, living his life in the limelight, were greater than those of many smaller and obscurer people. These mistakes were his undoing.

But his virtues were also those of a great man. He had great courage, both physical and moral. He was never afraid to risk his life, his freedom, his money, or his reputation. He had the pride of the strong; but though he had learned that it was a law of nature that the weak should go to the wall, he always fought on the side of the weak, the sick, and the oppressed. The only person toward whom he showed no pity was himself. By taking on the debts and troubles of others he died at an age when he should have been still in his prime. He was the victim of his own generosity.

This generosity was not a very humble quality. He was always taking on so much responsibility that he did not have time to give much more than money. He never had time to receive all those small tokens of love that make for friendship. And so he died, a sad and disillusioned man. It is true that it is more blessed to give than to receive. Jack London never allowed his friends the blessing of giving to him.

That was the tragedy of his private life. He turned the men and women who could have made his life rich with love and friendship into spongers by always giving and never receiving.

But Jack London, the writer, was quite a different person from that tired and disillusioned farmer and friend of the people who stopped breathing on November 22, 1916. The news of his death was flashed across a world locked in a bloody war in which every day thousands of British, French, Italian, German, Austrian, Turkish, Russian, and Greek soldiers were being killed and mourned.

In that war each nation had its own beloved casualties. In Britain, for example, the death of Rupert Brooke, the brilliant young poet killed not in action but by illness on active service, summed up the sacrifice of millions as young and fine but not so able to express themselves.

The death of Jack London at the age of forty cut across the battle lines. It shook people on both sides, because he stood for something larger than that war. He stood for a courage of mind and body that people believed would carry the twentieth century out of the mess and muck and poverty of the century before. When he died, millions felt that something of their own vigor, hope, adventure, and promise died with him. They had lived in his pages, and his sufferings and triumphs had been theirs.

But his dreams inspired them long after he was dead, different books at different times. Many people saw the Russian Revolution through his essay on *Revolution.* They saw prohibition through *John Barleycorn.* They saw the rise of Hitler in *The Iron Heel.* They saw Roosevelt's great new farming program through *The Valley of the Moon.*

Today Jack London's work as teacher has ended. But this only means that his real genius is all the clearer. He was a great artist. The short stories that he flung off at a thousand words a day, such as *To Build a Fire,* the animal stories *The Call of the Wild* and *White Fang,* and at least the novel *Martin Eden,* live because he was a great artist despite himself.

A NOTE ON BOOKS BY AND ABOUT JACK LONDON

JACK LONDON wrote out of his own experience more than most writers, but he was not concerned in telling the exact truth about himself so much as telling an effective story. The exception to this was *John Barleycorn,* which was an attempt to tell the truth about one part of his life, but only one part.

Charmian London wrote five books about Jack London and herself: *Jack London,* the official biography, and four travel books about Jack London in the South Seas. Her biography contains a great many interesting letters. But she was a bad writer and she was more interested in presenting herself in a good light than in discovering the truth about her husband.

In 1939, twenty-three years after Jack London died, but when many people who knew him were still alive, Irving Stone wrote *Sailor on Horseback.* This contained a great deal of fresh material, which is very useful. Unfortunately Irving Stone chose to sensationalize Jack London's life; although he corrected a number of Charmian London's mistakes, he introduced almost as many of his own.

The above books have all been used throughout this short life. Following are listed other books by Jack London which throw light on the particular chapter mentioned. The people who supplied information are also named.

Chapter One	Charmian Kittredge London and Irving Stone
Chapter Two	*John Barleycorn* and the above
Chapter Three	*The Cruise of the "Dazzler"*
Chapter Four	*The Cruise of the "Dazzler," Tales of the Fish Patrol*
Chapter Five	*The Sea Wolf, Martin Eden*
Chapter Six	*Martin Eden, The Road*
Chapter Seven	*Martin Eden*
Chapter Eight	*A Daughter of the Snows, The Son of the Wolf, The God of His Fathers, Children of the Frost,* etc.
Chapter Nine	*Martin Eden*
Chapter Ten	*The Kempton-Wace Letters, The Call of the Wild, The People of the Abyss*
Chapter Eleven	"The Yellow Peril" (reprinted in *Revolution*), "A Nose for the King" (in *When God Laughs*), *War Notes*
Chapter Twelve	*The Cruise of the "Snark,"* Martin Johnson, *Through the South Seas with Jack London*
Chapter Thirteen	*South Sea Tales, A Son of the Sun, The House of Pride, Martin Eden*
Chapter Fourteen	*The Mutiny of the "Elsinore"*
Chapter Fifteen	*The Valley of the Moon, The Little Lady of the Big House*